YOU ARE MINE

Drugged and held
in a secret bunker.
**This is my true story
of escape.**

ISABEL ERIKSSON

EBURY
PRESS

1 3 5 7 9 10 8 6 4 2

Ebury Press, an imprint of Ebury Publishing
20 Vauxhall Bridge Road
London SW1V 2SA

Ebury Press is part of the Penguin Random House group of companies
whose addresses can be found at global.penguinrandomhouse.com

Penguin
Random House
UK

This edition published by Ebury Press in 2018
First published in Sweden by Lind & Co in 2017

www.penguin.co.uk

A CIP catalogue record for this book is available from the British Library

ISBN 9781785037115

Typeset in India by Integra Software Services Pvt. Ltd, Pondicherry

Printed and bound in Great Britain by Clays Ltd, St Ives PLC

YOU ARE MINE

Although this book is based on real people and real events, names, places and identifying features have been changed in order to preserve their privacy.

I thought this book is intended to tell the students what to do more than to review the history and conventions of the perception they possess.

CONTENTS

The neighbour told us that he had lived in the area for more than fifty years. The house where Martin now lives was previously home to a family who kept horses. The spot that Martin built on used to be a paddock. The neighbour was asked whether he had helped Martin with the build. He explained that Martin had started work several years earlier. Martin had cast the various sections within the foundations himself. The neighbour had helped to erect the walls. After that, he wasn't allowed onto the site again.

SUMMARY OF INTERVIEW WITH MARTIN TRENNEBORG'S NEIGHBOUR

INTERROGATING OFFICER: *When did you start building?*

MARTIN TRENNEBORG: *I suppose it was about four years ago now.*

INTERROGATING OFFICER: *So you were having these thoughts as long as four years ago?*

MARTIN TRENNEBORG: *Correct.*

INTERROGATING OFFICER: *How many were you planning on locking up in this bunker?*

MARTIN TRENNEBORG: *How many people?*

INTERROGATING OFFICER: *Uh-huh.*

MARTIN TRENNEBORG: *Not sure. But more than one.*

[...]

INTERROGATING OFFICER: *And during this time, what did you say to Isabel about the fact that she was locked in this bunker? How did you explain it to her?*

MARTIN TRENNEBORG: *Well, that I had kidnapped her, simple as that.*

INTERROGATING OFFICER: *What else did you say?*

MARTIN TRENNEBORG: *That I wasn't going to hurt her.*

INTERROGATING OFFICER: *Did you tell her how long you were planning to hold her in there?*

MARTIN TRENNEBORG: *Yes, a long time, you could say.*

INTERROGATING OFFICER: *How long?*

MARTIN TRENNEBORG: *A number of years.*

[...]

INTERROGATING OFFICER: *Was it locked? Was she locked in the bunker?*

MARTIN TRENNEBORG: *She certainly was.*

INTERROGATING OFFICER: *What was Isabel's reaction to this?*

MARTIN TRENNEBORG: *Not great, I suppose. It made her sad, I guess.*

EXCERPT FROM POLICE INTERVIEW WITH
MARTIN TRENNEBORG, REFERRED TO BY
THE MEDIA AS 'THE BUNKER DOCTOR'

INTERROGATING OFFICER: *Did he say anything when you came to?*

ISABEL: *I was very tired and worn out, so probably still drugged. Then he told me that getting me unconscious took him much longer than he'd bargained for.*

EXCERPT FROM POLICE INTERVIEW WITH
ISABEL ERIKSSON

PROLOGUE

As I open my eyes, my body feels sluggish and stiff. As though it's struggling to keep up with the process of waking up.

Jeez, did I crash out?

I'm about to yawn and stretch when I'm struck by the realisation that it's not my ceiling I'm looking up at. Above me is a corrugated steel roof resting on light wooden joists. I blink hard a few times. It's cold here.

Here?

When I try to remember where I am, or what I was doing just before I fell asleep, or even what day it is, it just won't work. It's all so completely absurd and I really don't understand at all. Not only that, I can't think straight. It's as though my brain has turned to cotton wool. Something, though, is definitely wrong. *Very* wrong. I tear my eyes away from the strange ceiling and take a deep breath.

Jeans?

I'm lying under my own quilt, wearing my jeans and a thin pink top, but in a bed that isn't mine. When I roll over,

I can tell straight away that I'm not wearing any knickers underneath my trousers.

But I was wearing that blue dress, wasn't I?

My heart beats faster. That dress, yes. Images from my memory float to the surface, one by one, bursting like delicate bubbles while I try to take it all in and reconcile it with reality. The blue dress ... I was wearing it because I was going out to dinner? It was going to be a nice three-course meal and I was going to ... Then it hits me. Not *I, We*. I try to sit myself up but my body doesn't seem to want to oblige. My mouth's dry and my throat feels kind of thick. The smell of masonry dust is overpowering.

Nellie?

My seven-month-old toy poodle, who must've been lying curled up next to me, is suddenly very close, whimpering and trying to lick my face. Then she stiffens and stares out across the room. I say her name, to calm her down, and I'm surprised by how hoarse my voice is. Then I lift my head to see what she's looking at and my whole body turns ice-cold.

There's a man sitting there, on a stool, next to the bed. Instantly, the adrenaline courses through my veins and I swallow hard. He's just sitting there, staring at me. More bubbles float to the surface and then burst.

It's him. The American ...

I remember him from my apartment, was it ... yesterday? Or earlier today? I've no idea. The thought that I must've been so drunk that I fell asleep flashes past, but that can't be right either. And where am I? As I haul myself backwards in the bed to sit myself up and ask what the hell is going on, I feel a burning pain in my arm.

It fucking kills!

I manage to haul myself into a half-sitting position, and it feels almost as though I could do with a slap or two to get my head to clear. My eyes feel blurry and that's when I see the cannula sticking out of my forearm.

Am I in hospital?

Somehow, though, my consciousness has already clocked enough details for me to know that that isn't the case, and the panic strikes me like a punch in the chest. With tear-filled eyes I do the first thing that occurs to me: I grab hold of the thing stuck in my arm and pull as hard as I can. The pain as the cannula is torn from my vein is instant and intense. I drop what I've pulled out on to the bed and a few drops of blood smear across the sheets.

'That wasn't very well done,' says the man in the chair. The calmness of his voice brings a shiver to my core. 'It would've been better to let me do it. After all, I am a doctor.' His speech is slow, almost a kind of drawl.

Why is he speaking Swedish?

The man sitting on the chair is American, and he lives in London. We were going to have dinner with some of his colleagues. I was wearing my lovely blue dress ... My head spins and my breathing is getting faster and faster. I'm aware of Nellie pressing her little body closer to me. She's trembling, and growling quietly. Then I disappear off again.

Chapter One

THURSDAY

INTERROGATING OFFICER: *At what point did you decide you were going to drug her?*

MARTIN TRENNEBORG: *Hmm, that would've been on the Thursday, when we met for the first time.*

EXCERPT FROM INTERVIEW WITH
MARTIN TRENNEBORG

When I hear a knock on the door of the little studio apartment I'm renting in Östermalm, Stockholm, I've just finished freshening myself up after an enjoyable long walk in Tessinparken with Nellie. I look at the time, note that he's exceedingly punctual, and then glance around the room as I make my way over to the door. It's a lovely apartment on the first floor, decorated in a rustic style. The large windows look out onto an inviting courtyard and it's very handy for the open spaces around Djurgården and Gärdet.

Nellie barks, but doesn't run over to the door to greet our visitor – she's quite a timid little dog. I've laid out a cosy rug and a chew bone for her in the kitchen.

The man at the door is well built and he looks calm and self-confident as he smiles and introduces himself. He speaks English with a slight American accent. When we were arranging to meet, a couple of days ago, he told me that he was originally from America, but now lives in London, where he works in stocks and shares, and that he's in Stockholm on business for a few days. He's neatly dressed in a white shirt, braces and a smart suit.

'Come in,' I say once he's hung up his jacket in the hall, and I lead him towards the sofa. I've put my heels on and I'm making a concerted effort to make my movements as sensual as possible. Sitting on the sofa, I give him a glass of water and he eyes me up and down, then smiles – but it's not a creepy smile.

He says that if tonight goes well he'd like to book a whole night on Saturday, because he's going to a business dinner that he'd like me to come along to. All his Swedish colleagues will be there with their wives and he doesn't want to be the only one turning up without company.

'If you do come along, my date will definitely be the prettiest girl in the place,' he says with a wink.

I reply with a smile and tell him that it'll be no problem, then I ask him a few polite questions about his job.

We talk for a long time, about all sorts of things, including a fair bit about how the stock market operates, and he gives the impression of being respectable and intellectual. He thinks before he speaks, and when he does, the words emerge slowly, with a slight drawl. *This is not a man in a hurry*, I think to myself. He smells clean, I recognise his aftershave and he has a good posture.

'It'll be a three-course meal, and of course there will be lots of wine being served, but I was thinking maybe I could come here first?' He tentatively puts his hand on my knee. 'I can bring some nibbles and a half-bottle of champagne, so that we're in the mood by the time we get there.'

'Of course,' I reply. 'That's fine.'

'Dinner is at nine, so I thought I might come round at six?' He moves a bit closer to me. 'Then, after dinner, we can go back to my hotel, The Grand.'

Three hours ahead is a bit early, I think to myself. Even worse, Nellie's going to be on her own from nine at night until the following morning – I'll have to book her into a kennel.

'That'll be great,' I say, then I tell him how much it's going to cost.

He doesn't raise an eyebrow, just nods and then cocks his head to one side. 'A half-bottle of champagne should do it, right? I don't want to be too tipsy when we get to dinner. How would that look?'

I laugh politely, and his hand wanders from my knee up towards my thigh and I realise he's had enough of talking. As I'm wondering what to do with Nellie on Saturday, we move over onto the bed.

As soon as he's taken his underpants off, I notice he has a slight defect on his penis, like a little extra lump right down at the base. I ask him what it is. A lesson my first ever mentor taught me was always to inspect clients and make sure everything down there is normal, and even if it feels like a whole lifetime has passed since my first client I'm still very diligent about following that advice. Suddenly he recoils slightly and looks a bit embarrassed, then gives a short answer about it being an old injury from his time in the Military. It's obvious that he doesn't want to talk about it, and since it doesn't look like an STD, I leave the matter there and reach for a condom.

With him lying on top of me, in the missionary position, I feel the first – and only – weird vibe from this wealthy, calm, intellectual American. It's the way he looks me straight in the eye throughout. No, 'looks' isn't really the word. He downright stares into my eyes, all the time, in a way that is unusual and it unsettles me a bit. He has very intense green-blue eyes and the fact that he never looks away makes me feel exposed. Makes me feel more naked than getting undressed in front of any other client has ever made me feel. A thought flies through my consciousness, quick as a flash: *Psychopath Eyes.* I close mine, moan quietly, and try not to think about it too much, but then every time I open them, I'm confronted by his fixed, intense stare. Probing. So towards the end I mostly keep them closed, and think to myself what interesting little bedroom quirks people have.

Before long, he's finished. We lie there for a little while, then we decide that he'll be round at six on Saturday evening.

He's the perfect gentleman once more and he pays me several compliments. The thought of his intrusive, demanding stare soon evaporates from my mind. As I accompany him to the door he tells me how much he's looking forward to our meeting on Saturday. I reply that I feel the same way.

He turns in the doorway and thanks me once again, and gives me a kiss on the cheek.

I head straight for the kitchen to let Nellie out, then install myself in a hot shower. *The American turned out to be a good client*, I think to myself, and I'm looking forward to the meal on Saturday. But as I wash myself thoroughly in the rich suds, I am briefly taken back to that unsettling feeling I got from his staring eyes while we were having sex, but I shake it off. He was polite. There's no reason to give it any more thought. He is a client, the time he paid for is up, and as of now he has both come and gone.

I decide to have the next day off, and before I go to bed I arrange to meet a male friend of mine, a policeman, on Friday. I've known him for three years. It's been a while since we met up so we've got loads to catch up on. Tacos and a bottle of wine or two ... Watch a film, maybe a cheeseboard, and then talk for hours. It'll be lovely. The decision not to go to work the next day feels like the right one. In fact, it's a decision that seems to feel better each time I make it and I realise somehow that I've probably had enough of the escort lifestyle.

Maybe I'll make Saturday's booking my last?

Chapter Two

SATURDAY

INTERROGATING OFFICER: *So what happens on Saturday when you go round to her place?*

MARTIN TRENNEBORG: *Well, we have a pleasant evening, drinking champagne and I think I had a present with me too. And then ... ahem ... along with the champagne I'd brought some chocolate-dipped strawberries, which were drugged, so she falls asleep, you might say. And after that I take her out to my car just outside and drive her and her dog down south, to Skåne.*

INTERROGATING OFFICER: *Right. What was it that you drugged her with?*

MARTIN TRENNEBORG: *Something called flunitrazepam, would you like me to spell that for you?*

EXCERPT FROM POLICE INTERVIEW WITH
MARTIN TRENNEBORG

On Saturday morning I wake up in an enormous house in Djursholm. Friday hadn't quite gone according to plan, but it had still gone really well. My friend, the policeman, got in touch – he couldn't make it, and since I was pretty sick of working I decided to arrange to meet Björn, a guy I met on Tinder. He's a young lawyer, well on the way to becoming a barrister, and living in this fantastic pad. I remember thinking there must be several apartments in the building, but it turned out the whole place was his. Björn is lively, intelligent and good-looking, and we ate and drank well before we ended up in bed together.

As I sit up in the luxurious bed I can hear clanking coming from the kitchen. When I come down, Björn has laid on a delicious breakfast for us to eat together out on the beautiful terrace, and we chat about maybe seeing each other again. He doesn't know what I do – I told him I was a make-up artist – and, as usual, my guilty conscience is gnawing away at me for having to tell lies. I visualise what life might be like if I was to get together with Björn: if we lived together, in this beautiful house by the water. Some of the most expensive houses in Stockholm are in this very neighbourhood. *Barrister's wife* ... That has a nice ring to it, but I have to be honest – that genuine spark isn't really there. I'd probably have had a more rewarding evening last night if my male friend hadn't rearranged. We've decided to meet up on Tuesday instead. I'm looking forward to that.

After Björn has given me a lift home I take Nellie out for a long walk. It's a warm, sunny day; summer has yet to finally release its grip on Stockholm and I find myself laughing out loud, getting great pleasure out of seeing my gawky young dog playing in the grass and chasing colourful butterflies. A little while later, we come to a riding club I've never seen before, only about a fifteen-minute walk from my apartment. There's a girl having a private lesson in one of the paddocks and I stop and watch for a while. The horse's taut muscles rippling in the sunshine are fascinating and seductive, and I'm struck by an intense desire to have a horse of my own again when I notice the familiar, musty scent of the stables. A bit further on, three people are having a showjumping lesson and I end up staying there even longer. I pull a long straw from the grass, start chewing it and prop myself up against the fence, my arms perched on top of it. The turf flies from under the horse's hooves as both horse and rider ready themselves and then leap over the obstacles.

The other life is pulling at me. The one where I can be honest about what I do, all the time. *A life on horseback …* I feel a great longing, deep inside. The only thing standing between me and that other life is a conscious decision. I can certainly afford a good horse. Nellie – who until now has been staring in awe at what I imagine to her must appear to be enormous dogs – starts whining; she probably thinks we've been standing here for too long. I bend over and absentmindedly stroke her behind the ear.

Maybe that's what I should do, I think to myself. *Buy a manageable-sized stable, break in a few horses each year, and maybe combine it with a day kennel?* Obviously the income it would generate wouldn't be anything like what I earn now, but I do think it would bring me a different kind of happiness. Now Nellie's standing up on her hind legs, with her front paws patting against my legs, whimpering again and wagging her tail. She makes me laugh.

'Okay, poppet, let's go,' I say, promising myself to investigate this option more thoroughly. At that very moment, one of the horses whinnies happily behind me and I take that as a sign. The weather, the horses, Nellie and the freedom I've got to decide my own future make me happy, and then when everyone I meet as we walk on seems to be wearing a friendly smile, I realise that I'm walking around beaming myself.

On the way home I stop off at a sushi bar and order teppanyaki duck with rice. You never know what these dinners will be like and besides we're going to share a little bottle of champagne beforehand. I sit down in the warm sunshine and tuck in, with Nellie curled up in my lap. I give her a few tastes, which she gobbles down hungrily while squinting into the sun. Even though it's hot, you can smell autumn in the air. Right here, right now, I am happy.

The phone rings, a number I don't recognise. It's the American, just calling to check we're still on for tonight, at six.

'Yes, that suits me,' I say as I pop the last bit of duck in my mouth.

'I wonder,' he says, suddenly sounding a little unsure, 'whether maybe we could spend the night at yours, rather than back at my hotel? This restaurant where we're eating is only five minutes from your place.'

SATURDAY

That would be great, I think to myself – *not least since I still haven't had the chance to make arrangements for Nellie.* So that's what we settle on. When I get home I log in to Facebook, click the *feeling free* emoticon and update my status: *What's next?*

*

Since we're going to have dinner in a fancy restaurant, I'm dressed up a bit more than the last time I met the American. I've gone for a beautiful blue evening dress, one that glitters gently in the right light. It's sexy, but classy. Short, but not too short. Figure-hugging in all the right places, yet not too revealing. Underneath I'm wearing a pair of new black nylon stockings and some sexy underwear. I've cleaned the apartment, done the washing up, dimmed the lighting and lit some tea lights. An expensive scented candle fills the room with an unmistakably sensual air. The vase in the middle of the table is bursting with gorgeous pink flowers I picked up on the way home and the whole scene is sound-tracked by some unobtrusive background music. I walk past the mirror in the hall a few times to reassure myself that both my hair and my make-up are just right.

When, as the clock strikes six, there's still no sign of my client, it does occur to me that he might have got cold feet and decided not to come after all. Clients usually make sure they arrive on time, but we've already met once so he's probably just been held up.

At twelve minutes past six the doorbell rings and there he is. Once again, he's very well dressed; his demeanour is calm and composed. Inside, he thrusts a gift towards me. It's perfume and the wrapping is covered in tiny white and pink flowers that he says he has picked himself. I'm moved, foolishly so. Clients do occasionally give me presents, everything from jewellery to flowers, but always bought – perhaps that's their way of showing me how wealthy they are. But picking the flowers himself? I think that's really sweet and I tell him so. He smiles and passes me an envelope containing my cash fee – sixteen thousand kronor (about nineteen hundred pounds) for the night. I count it – just to make sure – then put it away.

'I've brought some chocolate-dipped strawberries,' he says.

I struggle to place his American accent. *Maybe that's because he's been in London for so long*, I think, and then I lead him over to the fridge so that he can put the bowl of strawberries in there until he's opened the champagne. I grab a couple of glasses. He tells me how beautiful I look and then we sit down on the sofa and start chatting away while we sip on the bubbly. I've always liked champagne but I have to keep reminding myself not to drink too quickly. We're going to be here for near enough three hours and there isn't going to be any sex before dinner.

He doesn't give any hint of being nervous as he tells me more about his job, giving me plenty of tips if ever I were to look at investing in shares. At one point he gets his phone out and shows me a few websites – really exclusive escort agencies in London, ones he thinks I should work for if ever I decide to live there. He seems to be very well informed about which ones are best. As we chat away, my thoughts turn to the evening's dinner. I'm looking forward to it, wondering what they might serve and what the American's colleagues will make of me. Will they know I'm an escort? When I ask him about his colleagues and their wives, his answers are short and snappy, almost irritated. I ask him again – maybe we should get our story straight about how we met or something like that, so that his colleagues don't get suspicious? But he just gets annoyed again. It's obvious that he doesn't want to talk about it and I don't want to seem nosy so I settle for the little he does say. His response makes me feel a bit uneasy, but it's easy enough to shrug off. Apart from that, he's a nice guy. *Que sera, sera* . . .

It gets to nearly eight o'clock, by which time we've been talking for almost two hours when he says it's time for the strawberries, and that he might feel like a nap after we've had them. I think it's a bit late for that, dinner being only an hour away, but he does look a bit tired and I know that even fifteen minutes' sleep can work wonders if you're feeling a bit fuzzy.

He picks up our glasses while I grab the bowl of strawberries from the fridge. I put them on the bedside table on his side of the bed and snuggle up so that I'm sort of half-lying down alongside him. I'm relaxed and really looking forward to a great meal in sophisticated company. He looks at his watch a few times and seems to be getting more and more nervous as the dinner approaches. Maybe there's some crucial deal at stake?

When he picks up a strawberry and dangles it in front of my mouth, it feels like a scene from a sensual film and I can see that he wants to feed me. I take a bite and it tastes like chocolate-dipped strawberries always do – heavenly. He eats one himself, then feeds me another. We carry on talking. I realise that I am actually a bit peckish so I devour the strawberries at the same rapid rate as he offers them. Every now and then he takes one himself, but I end up having by far the lion's share. At one point it does occur to me that maybe I should feed him one too, but quickly realise I haven't the energy. In fact, I'm starting to feel . . .

'Are you a bit tired?' the American asks, stroking my arm.

'Mmhmm . . .' I reply and have a bit of a stretch.

This isn't like me. Where did this tiredness come from? I've hardly drunk anything, not even a whole glass of champagne, in over two hours.

'Me too,' he whispers. Then he pats himself on the chest. 'I want you to lie down here,' he says.

I cannot resist. The tiredness has found its way into every part of my body and it now feels like I wouldn't be able to stay awake even if I wanted to. Somewhere, an alarming sensation flashes past, the feeling that something is very, *very* wrong, but I don't manage to grab hold of it.

'I'm going to have a little sleep too,' he says.

That makes all the other thoughts disappear. I lay my head on the American's chest.

Then I'm out.

*

I come round. It feels like I'm ... moving?

Am I sitting up?

For a couple of seconds, I'm aware that I'm sitting in the front seat of a car, with Nellie on my lap, and I'm wrapped up in my duvet.

What's going on?

Then everything goes black again.

*

Without knowing how it's happened, or how much time has passed, I realise that I'm standing up. The floor is cold. Dusty. Dry. But I still don't recognise my surroundings. *Where am I? Am I dreaming?*

The American is standing there in front of me, between me and an open door. That's weird, because I just heard a heavy door slam shut. The feeling of unreality is about to take over again.

'What's going on? Who are you? I'm so cold,' I manage as I take a stumbling step towards the man.

He sighs.

'Martin,' he replies slowly, as if talking to a foolish child. 'You already know this. Maybe it is a little bit cold in here, but your shivering is mainly down to the rush of adrenaline. You really should lie down and get some more rest – you shouldn't be standing up, wandering around. Not yet.'

Martin, yes. He's a doctor. And he talks like one too.

My jaw trembles and the corners of my mouth sink towards the floor; my right arm hurts and the inside of my elbow is bruised black and blue. The panic returns as it dawns on me that he must have drugged me. The door behind him is the only way out of this nightmare and he's not planning to get out of the way.

'You …' My voice cracks and I have to stop, clear my throat and try again. 'What have you done to me? You can't keep me here. You have to let me go!'

Nellie starts barking from the bed in response to my raising my voice.

Martin gives her an angry look, then looks over at me again. *How can he be so calm? Doesn't he understand what he's doing?*

'Noooo … sooooorry,' he says, drawing the words out. 'I'm not going to let you go. It took longer than I'd bargained – to get you unconscious, I mean,' he goes on, as if that were the most natural thing in the world. 'I'm planning to keep you here for a couple of years or so.'

My ears pop as the blood rushes to my head. I clench my fists. Suddenly I'm reeling around the place and my legs almost give way. I take a look around: the space is grey, dusty and messy, like a small garage or a building site. Or like a shelter, a … a …

A bunker.

The implications of what Martin has just said now hit me head-on: he has kidnapped me. Somehow he has managed to drug me and brought me to this place, a specially built bunker. And he's planning to keep me here. *To have me as though I was just some pet. For a couple of years?*

I can't breathe properly and my head is in turmoil. *I can't stay here with him in captivity. It's not happening, I need to get out!*

On a shelf close to me there are two long screws so I reach out to grab them, raising my hands and making a noise like a crazed animal, and I notice my upper lip has curled up, showing my teeth. *Who the* fuck *does he think he is? Anger.* Boiling with rage, I gather as much strength as I can from the fury.

I am going to kill him.

My steps, though, are not as purposeful as my intent. My body isn't playing along and it ends up being a bungling attempt at attack, which he easily deflects simply by grabbing hold of my wrists, hard. I realise that I don't have any strength at all to resist with. He easily pushes my arms down and wrestles the screws from my hands, despite my best efforts. It hurts when he uses brute force to prise open my tightly clenched fists. Almost as much as it hurts to realise: *This man has drugged and abducted me. Locked me in a bunker, God knows where, and he's planning to keep me here.* No one knows where I am, or even that I was going to meet him. Or had I mentioned it to anyone? Now my head's spinning again and the last drops of energy I have managed to muster desert me. I collapse in a heap on the floor, exhausted, sobbing; trying to understand. The next thing that pops into my head is: Fritzl. And that guy in America, the one who had three young girls locked in his house for years – he kept them as sex slaves. I wrap my arms around my knees and start rocking gently back and forth. With the tears streaming down my face I look up at the man who has kidnapped me. The fear rips at my back with long claws. I'm completely terrified. *What is he planning to do? Rape me? Torture me?* 'A couple of years' – those were his exact words. *Then what? Murder me, once he's tired of me? Has he held someone else captive before me? And if he has, what happened to her?* The panic feels like a huge flock of birds flying around my insides, violently crashing into each other and squawking away.

'Oh my God, oh my God, oh my God!' I hear someone wail. I realise that it's me and bite hard on the inside of my cheeks to try to put an end to the chaos inside my body. I haul myself backwards on my backside, as far away from this monster as possible. After only a couple of metres I can go no further and the tears are threatening to drown me. I curl up into a ball to make myself as small as possible. My teeth are chattering.

This is not happening. This is not happening. This is not happening.

But Martin is standing over me, perfectly calm and with a cold, dead look in his eyes. 'Don't do that again,' he tells me.

Deep down I realise there is probably no point, yet still I start screaming for help, as loud as I possibly can. I scream and scream and scream and scream that I am here, that someone has to help me; that I am going to die. At this Nellie loses it altogether and barks so persistently over there on the bed that it sounds like she too is crying out for help.

What finally gets me to stop is that Martin doesn't react at all, nor does he make any attempt whatsoever to get me to stop. On the contrary, he looks almost entertained by it. I go quiet; I snort mucus down my throat and try to dry the tears that just will not stop. My throat is on fire ...

'It's no good,' he says, when Nellie has finally gone quiet. 'You can scream as loud as you like – no one's going to hear you. And if you do try to escape again, I will chain you to the bed and give you nothing but bread and water.' He seems to be mulling that over, consulting with himself while drumming his fingertips against his bottom lip. 'Well, I'd have to come and unchain you when you need to use the toilet, of course.' Then he laughs. 'But then again you didn't have any complaints about your nappy on the journey down.'

With those words, he turns around and leaves. The door slams behind him and I hear a series of clicking noises.

Hold my breath.

I hear another door. My heart stops.

Two doors?

Then, as I hear a *third* door closing, the tears start to flow once more.

Chapter Three

SUNDAY

MARTIN TRENNEBORG: *The thing about the mask was ... that was something I said so that ... maybe this sounds a bit cruel, but ... to make sure she didn't get her hopes up that someone might've seen her. She had all sorts of ideas. That someone might be tracking the car via GPS and things like that. Not particularly realistic, is it? She was convinced they could find her, right where she was, which of course was not the case.*

INTERROGATING OFFICER: *So when she said this, did you answer her? When she brought up the idea that somebody might be able to track her down, to the bunker, via GPS and all the rest of it?*

MARTIN TRENNEBORG: *Yes, I told her ... well, I told her that it wasn't very realistic.*

EXCERPT FROM POLICE INTERVIEW WITH
MARTIN TRENNEBORG

I woke up in this awful place, in this ... *bunker*. I've torn a cannula out of my own arm and the inside of my elbow is caked in blood. I've tried overpowering the 'American' – who turns out to be a Swedish doctor called Martin – with two long screws and failed miserably. And now I have heard three doors slam shut as he left, leaving me all alone again.

A while later, I've no idea how long, the tears stop flowing. All I can hear is the sound of my own breathing. Rapid, fluttering, like a butterfly's wings. Panicked. Beyond that, nothing but foreboding silence. Nellie comes over to me and whines softly, so I pick her up and bury my face in her thick coat. I'm sort of grateful to have her with me, but at the same time I'm terrified of what that psychopath might do to her ... and to me. Somehow I push those thoughts away and haul myself up from the floor. I strain to see my surroundings. The worst of the haziness has gone, but my body still feels stiff and slow. I shiver as I drop Nellie onto the bed, then look around: the bunker is grey and bleak, blank walls, just plasterboard on concrete. The floor isn't finished. There's a thick layer of brick dust on every surface and the ceiling is made of corrugated steel. I stand on the bed and slam my fist into it so hard my knuckles hurt. It makes a bit of noise, but not as much as I'd expected. There's something above the metal – concrete perhaps.

Am I underground?

For a few seconds that thought makes it hard to breathe and the panic wants to break out again when I realise that I have absolutely no idea where I am. No idea whether I'm still in Stockholm ... or even Sweden. Or what day it is today.

How long was I out for?

Instinctively, I start looking for my phone, but of course it's nowhere to be seen. The hopelessness I feel inside is threatening to completely take over. But I clench my teeth and compose myself – I refuse to accept there is no way out.

Alongside the bed there's a table and two chairs. I try to move around as quietly as humanly possible. I don't know whether or not *he* can hear me, but I don't want to make him angry. That could cost me my life.

The only lighting in here is a bulkhead lamp over in the corner and the brick dust in the air swirls like tornados in its stark light. Still sniffling, I look for something on the table that I might be able to use to get out of here. Out of nowhere, the urge to vomit overwhelms me and I clutch my stomach as it takes hold. *Those flowers ... They're the same kind he'd brought to my place. The ones he'd picked himself and I'd thought that was so cute.* I just want to slam the vase against the wall and scream, but I hold it together for Nellie's sake. It would only scare her even more. I need to hold it together, for her sake. Think. Get us out of here!

Is anyone looking for me?

The tears well up, burning the insides of my eyelids. I'm supposed to be having brunch with Nathalie on Sunday, and then I was going to meet my friend, the policeman, on Tuesday. If I don't show up, and he can't get hold of me, maybe he'll start ... something? An investigation? Perhaps my mum, or my sister, have tried to contact me and are getting worried now? But then again, it might only have been a few hours since he kidnapped me, in which case no one will have noticed that I'm not there. Whichever it is, there's probably not a single person on the planet that knows where I am right now. Not even me.

A feeling of unbearable isolation rolls through my chest; wave upon wave of grief and terror. I do my best not to let the fear get the better of me and blink the tears away.

There's a worktop along one wall, complete with a kitchen sink and a few utensils scattered across it. I can't say for certain, but it feels like there were more things there earlier ... last time I woke up. Between the worktop and the table is a doorway, with two hinges sticking out on one side. I steady myself with one hand against the wall as I peer through. My hands are flecked with grey and the dirt has found its way under my fingernails. It's very dark in there – but it looks like another, smaller room. There are a few loose planks propped up against the far wall.

At the far end of the bunker, immediately to the right of the door that Martin disappeared through, are sacks of cement, a shower that hasn't been plumbed in and two toilet pans.

Two?

A shiver runs through me.

Beyond that, it's pitch-black, so I don't get any further.

The sight of the shower awakens a desire to get clean. My jeans are rubbing at the crotch and ... That's when it hits me. The last thing I remember is that we were going to eat strawberries. We were lying on the bed. It must've been then that he drugged me. And … I was wearing that blue dress. But now I've got jeans on … With no knickers. That means he's undressed me. Why?

I know why, whispers a horrible voice from the darkest recesses of my consciousness. *The trousers are rubbing at the crotch and that's because I'm not wearing any knickers. Because he's taken them off when I was out cold. Did he rape me?*

I'm overcome with rage and grief at the same time. *This man has taken the liberty of stripping me naked while I was unconscious. Defenceless. Completely without a voice. God knows what else he's done to me.* Nellie can tell I'm getting more and more upset and she starts whimpering. I walk back towards the bed, scratch her behind the ears and just as I'm about to say something comforting … a noise.

I freeze.

Is it him? Or someone else? Someone who could save me? I fill my lungs to scream, but then hear the sound of the outer door slamming. *It's him! He's back. What's he going to do now?* My whole body starts shaking and when he finally enters the room I'm sitting on the edge of the bed with Nellie in my arms.

As he gets closer I notice he's got something in his hand. I don't know where to look. *Is he going to get angry if I stare at him? Or if I don't look at him?* Even after all the things I've been through, nothing could ever have prepared me for anything like this and I am absolutely terrified. The fear is relentless, like a stubborn, evil shadow.

He doesn't say a word. Just keeps staring at me with those cold, blue-green eyes as he pulls up a chair and sits down next to the bed. Each one of his movements is calm and precise; he has a manner that makes my skin crawl. He then throws something onto the bed next to me and I have to bite my cheeks to stop myself from screaming out loud. I stare at it: a little notebook and pen. He lifts his head.

'Write down what sort of food you want me to get you.' He runs his tongue across his front teeth and smacks his lips. 'You know, breakfast and snacks and stuff.'

I don't even bother to reply; it's just too fucked up. Every now and then, I find myself thinking this probably isn't even really happening; that it *has* to be a nightmare. *Am I supposed to just sit here and write a shopping list for my kidnapper?*

A great torrent of four-letter words rushes towards my lips but I manage to stifle it. I have no idea how this man works; what makes him angry; how he behaves then. Whether or not he's prone to violence. And what's worse, I am completely at his mercy.

Martin sighs. 'For your own good, you should try to grasp this straight away. There's no point resisting or being difficult, or giving me this silent treatment. I don't want to hurt you. I want you to enjoy life as much as possible, for as long as you are here.' He nods towards the notebook and pen again. 'Write down any books you'd like too, so it doesn't get too boring.'

'And then what?' I manage.

He then takes a deep breath and looks relieved that I'm at least talking to him. 'As I said, I don't want to hurt you, I want you to have a nice time here. As far as possible, under the circumstances, I mean. Naturally I understand that ...' He goes quiet, as though negotiating with himself. Crosses one leg over the other. 'Listen, okay, I *will* let you go. I am going to do that.'

The hope I feel is like a red, glowing ember being lit in my belly and the heat gradually spreads through my body.

'When?' I whisper.

He rocks his head back and forth a few times, almost as though he is totting it up. 'A couple of years ... or so?'

The ember that was glowing is immediately extinguished and replaced with anger. I take a breath and prepare to object but he raises his hand to cut me off: 'It is not my intention to hurt you, Isabel.'

How the fuck does he know my real name?

'I want you to have a nice time here, at my place. I think that if you ... well ... if you just give it a chance, you might even start to like it ... me.'

Everything I was about to say falls flat. How do you respond to something like that? How sick is this guy? He says he doesn't want to hurt me, apparently oblivious to the fact that he already has. Doesn't he realise that depriving someone of their liberty *is* hurting them? Drugging, then kidnapping her, taking her away from everything she cares about? Locking her up, against her will, without anyone knowing where she is and then telling her she's going to be there for a couple of years? How can he think that's 'not hurting' me? He must be really, really sick. And he said my real name. That means he went through all my personal stuff while I was unconscious. The fear starts growing again and my stomach clenches, although I try not to show it – I don't want to show weakness.

'How long is a couple of years?' I ask.

He shrugs and gives me a look that says it doesn't really matter. 'I don't know, just a couple of years. Then I'm going to let you go.'

Somehow it does come as a relief when he says that. Until he adds: 'Maybe.'

He smiles and nods towards the pen and paper again.

Maybe? What does that mean? That it might be a couple of years, or he might not let me go at all? If he doesn't, he'll have to . . . My head is spinning; I feel like I'm going to pass out. As far as I can make out, there are only two alternatives to his letting me go: either he keeps me locked up for the rest of my life, or else he kills me once he gets bored. That's the most likely scenario, surely? He must know that if I ever do get out of here, I'll be heading straight for the nearest police station.

'Where am I?' I ask. Not having a clue about that makes everything even more twisted. More nightmarish.

'At my place,' he replies slowly.

'But, *where?*' I insist.

His response is just a sigh.

Regardless of all that even if I remember absolutely nothing, could a man transporting a lifeless body really have gone completely unnoticed? For a second, the moment I came round flashes before me. I was sitting wrapped in my duvet, with Nellie on my knee. Was I in a car at that point? I suddenly remember him telling me that I'd had a nappy on for the journey.

Martin frowns. 'How much do you remember?'

I just want to scream at him, tell him to fuck right off ... Demand he let me go ... Hit him over the head with something solid ... I manage to keep my cool though, and just say: 'Nothing. I remember us eating strawberries and me getting tired.'

He clears his throat and adjusts his position on the chair. 'Well then, one thing at a time: you're at my place, I built this with my own hands.' As he says this, he looks around with a look of pride on his face that makes me want to puke. 'Five years, it took me. I've ploughed an awful lot of time and money into this, Isabel. Making sure that everything was ... just right.'

At this I feel even more nauseous. Frustration makes me pick at the quicks of my fingernails and they soon start bleeding. The adrenaline is pumping through my body once again.

'For example, there have been others ... well, people who've tried ... things like this. In America, you know? They made the mistake of making it too easy for the girls to escape. Here –' he points towards the door with his arm fully extended '– I've installed three doors.'

He goes quiet and it looks like he's waiting for me to say something along the lines of *wow!* It takes all the self-control

I can muster not to just scream out loud. When I say nothing, he goes on: 'Three doors, the sort of thing you'd have in a bank vault. They weigh over three hundred kilos each. Then an awful lot of concrete and cement. No one's getting through these walls, not even with the proper equipment. Two of the doors have combination locks and of course I'm the only one who knows the codes.' He points to some pipes hanging from the ceiling. 'Still, the ventilation is outstanding – better than in a lot of modern houses. I've done everything myself from the ground up. Obviously I had to do it myself, otherwise people might've wondered. The water comes from my own borehole and I've even done all the electrics myself. It wasn't easy, but I pick things up quickly, I suppose.' The pride in his voice is obvious.

My teeth are chattering again and I pull the duvet around me, just as Nellie hops down onto the floor.

'Nellie,' I call after her, but she runs off into a corner and starts sniffing around. I recognise these signs and my blood runs cold. 'Nellie, no!' I say, slightly louder. She crouches down in the corner and proceeds to pee onto a plank. Throughout she keeps her eyes firmly fixed on Martin, as if she can tell he's dangerous.

Martin wrinkles his nose. 'Hmm. That could be ... a problem,' he says slowly, each word drawn out. As though he's working out how to deal with it, and I really don't want to know which alternative courses of action are going through his mind. Back at home Nellie has just been house-trained, so I've been careful to make sure she gets out regularly and to give her lots of praise when she's done her thing – but here? Where's she supposed to go? It almost breaks my heart, the thought of her being trapped here, in these miserable few square metres, and not seeing the sun for a couple of years. I call her again and once she's finished, she pads back over. I pick her up and then hold her tightly to my chest.

'I'll have to think of something,' Martin says. 'Anyway, as I'm sure you'll have worked out, this place is also completely soundproof ...' He lets that sentence peter out.

There is one question I can't let go of, I just have to ask: 'Are we ... underground?'

He bursts into a loud fit of surprised, incredulous laughter, as though it's the most ridiculous thing he's heard in ages. 'Under ...? No, no, we're not.'

Somehow that, in spite of everything, gives me a weird sense of relief. He quickly adds: 'That doesn't actually matter, in the circumstances. You might as well be. As I said, you can scream as much as you like, no one's going to hear any of it. You could stage a rock concert in here and no one would be any the wiser. You're not going to be able to escape either, so there's really no point in trying.' His mood suddenly darkens. 'And about that little ... attack earlier ... That's not a good idea either. I've taken a few things away, things that were in here before. A few large, heavy things, I've taken them in case you get it into your head to try to hurt me again. And if you do, you will be punished. I'd also like you to know that I am a former elite soldier so you really don't have a hope. But then

35

you did actually try to kill me before, with those screws. You came close to my throat, it could've all gone so badly wrong.'

He looks hurt. As though *I'm* the one who's done something wrong. My guts wrap themselves into a tight knot. At least I know why it feels emptier in here – he's removed a load of stuff to protect himself from *me*. In his sick, twisted world *he* is the one who needs protection. *Did he move it all without my hearing a sound? Did he drug me again somehow? Surely I would have noticed it otherwise.*

'It's not altogether finished yet,' he goes on, nodding towards the planks piled up in one corner. 'And it's a bit dusty. But once it's all finished, the floor and everything, it's going to be great.'

'They will find me,' I say quietly. So quietly in fact that it's barely audible. I stare down at Nellie's thick coat – I cannot bear to meet his eyes.

'No,' he says simply, perfectly calm.

'Yes, they will.'

'And how do you think that might happen?' It sounds as though he's vaguely entertained by the idea.

'My mobile phone. Satellites. My friends and family are going to notice I'm missing and then they can track all that . . .'

He snorts, a condescending chuckle. 'That isn't very realistic. I have taken care of your phone. Naturally I turned it off so that it could not be traced. Do you really think I would overlook such a crucial detail? And this thing about people . . . you're going to give me your passwords – Facebook, emails and so on. But we'll come back to that.'

36

Despite my best efforts, my hands refuse to stop trembling, so I clutch them to my stomach. 'Somebody must've seen you. As you were ... taking me away.'

He laughs again. 'You don't seem to appreciate how much careful planning has gone into this. No one has seen me do anything with you. Both of us were wearing masks, real Hollywood masks. We looked like an old couple – one driving, the other in a wheelchair. Perfectly normal. So, no, no one has seen anything. No one is going to trace you – you might as well get used to it.'

I can't hold back the tears any longer, but I do at least try to cry quietly – I don't want to give him the satisfaction of seeing me lose it altogether. It does seem as though my tears have some effect on him, because he jumps to his feet.

'I'm going to get something to eat. You should really have a rest for a while.' After a couple of paces he turns around: 'Are you a good cook?'

It's an absurd question, but I answer anyway. I tell it like it is – I mostly eat takeaways. So no, I'm not a particularly good cook.

He pauses for a moment, staring at me. Then another snigger. 'Oh well,' he states calmly. 'You'll be able to teach yourself now. You could even do a bit of studying while you're here, read a load of books and educate yourself. Train to be something. I mean, you've got plenty of time on your hands.'

And with that, he leaves me alone in the bunker once more.

*

Once the last of the doors has slammed to, I let go and cry inconsolably into Nellie's thick coat. Things that Martin said to me are spinning around inside my head and I still feel pretty woozy after having been unconscious for so long.

He's kidnapped me. Now he tells me that I'm going to be here for a couple of years. It's all too much to take in and the panic starts bubbling up inside me again. Even though I can't recall the last time I actually had anything to drink, I can feel that my bladder is full. As much as I don't want to, I realise that I *need* to go to the toilet.

Martin has built a screening wall in the middle of the bunker, behind which there is a toilet, a tiny sink on the wall and a toilet brush. When I get to my feet, Nellie darts straight over to the door that Martin has just walked through, whines and gives me a look that tells me she's had enough of this place; that it really is high time to go home. Seeing the disappointment in her eyes as I head for the toilet instead of the door is heart-wrenching.

The toilet pan is perched on a few wooden planks. One of them is loose so I pull it out and swing it through the air. I imagine myself standing here, hidden by the wall; hearing him approach and then whacking him over the head for all I'm worth. But what would that achieve? There would still be three doors between me and freedom. I put the plank back where I found it and inspect the toilet – for a moment I wonder if it's even plumbed in, but then I lift the lid and see that it is indeed full of water. The seat is unsteady so I sit down carefully and do what I have to do. I stare at the door throughout. There's a keypad, where you have to enter the code to get out. Maybe I can sneak a peek when he leaves?

And then what? He's just told me that two of the doors have codes.

My throat tightens. Tears roll as I stretch to reach the toilet roll balanced on the sink. There's a bottle of soap on there too. I look down at my hands: they're filthy, dirt under my nails, split quicks. My hair feels dry and dirty, and the odour from between my legs as I wipe makes me grimace.

The water in the tap is ice-cold but I persevere and wash my hands and face. This helps, makes me feel sharper. Nellie barks and jumps up against my leg.

'Oh, poppet, sorry, you must be parched,' I say and head for the kitchen sink. I find a little plastic bowl, fill it with water and Nellie jumps on it as though she's found a crock of gold. My heart breaks for the umpteenth time.

I want to go home.

***

Just north of Gothenburg, on Sweden's west coast, lies the town of Uddevalla. I was born there, a little over thirty years ago. We lived out in the country, in a big house with a gym, sauna and a lovely big garden. Uddevalla was a good place to grow up. Since the sixteenth century it has burned to the ground no fewer than six times and the town has switched nationality on seven occasions since then. So as you can imagine, ruffling the feathers of an Uddevalla native is no easy task. Famous sons and daughters include engineering magnate Percy Barnevik, renowned commentator Agneta Klingspor, football ace Martin Dahlin, singer Sylvia Vrethammar, as well as the world's first supermodel, Lisa Fonssagrives-Penn. For a small town, there's a reasonable cultural scene, sport and commerce. The town's most famous industry used to be a match factory, but it closed in 1938. Perhaps they were looking to avoid any more major fires.

As a child, I spent a lot of time daydreaming. Mum tells me that I was a kind child – that I barely argued with my big sister – but that I was no stranger to a bit of mischief and I was always keen to try out my ideas, some of which weren't great. I guess that comes with the vivid imagination.

Ever since I was little I've been the enterprising type and I've always wanted to run my own business, because Dad did. I was always in his office, asking him to explain what the paperwork was all about.

I loved spending time in the great outdoors and we often took day trips as a family – picnics in a forest, long rambles, hoping to catch sight of some wild animal. Also a homebody, I loved family life and I was only too happy to help out at home: folding laundry, washing up and, above all, baking – I loved it. When I grew up, I decided, I was going to be an astronaut *and* run a kennel for breeding small dogs, *as well as* having a modelling career and doing something to do with make-up.

Even though I was quite a shy child, I was adventurous and inventive. My room was a mess, full of toys, and according to Mum I was more fearless than other kids. I had none of those fears that children usually have – neither darkness nor monsters under the bed caused me any concern. If we ever saw a scary film, my sister would be the one gripping a cushion, ready to hide her face behind it if it got too much, not me. That lack of fear is something I think I carried into adulthood.

*

To be perfectly honest, I was never very conscientious at school. I've never been much of a bookworm either, and I never liked studying stuff that didn't interest me. I always got average grades though, so it wasn't as if I neglected it altogether.

My social life consisted mainly of hanging out with my female friends – there were five of us in our gang and we spent most of our time together. Aside from that, I remained pretty shy throughout my first years at school, but I put that down to the glasses I had to wear at the time – I really hated them. God, how I loathed those specs! They were the jam-jar type that really magnified my eyes and made me look like a freak. So when I was sixteen, I finally plucked up the courage to say no to glasses and got myself some contact lenses instead. I haven't worn glasses since and I have never regretted it, not for one second. All of a sudden boys were noticing me. I started getting compliments from friends and even teachers too. It gave my self-confidence a real boost.

As a schoolgirl, my two biggest idols were undoubtedly Swedish show jumper Malin Baryard and celebrity entrepreneur and reality TV pioneer Paris Hilton. The former is probably no surprise – I was a horses' kind of girl and as soon as any kind of equestrian sport came on the television I would sit there glued to it. The whole family travelled down to the Gothenburg Horse Show several times so that I could see the jumpers live, and getting to experience the whole thing first hand was fantastic. I dreamed of a future where I myself would get to ride in major competitions.

Paris Hilton caught my imagination as a teenager. I saw the life she lived – the luxury, the excess. She seemed to do so much travelling, something I badly wanted to do myself. And of course she always had the best clothes and bags. It might have been then that I first started dreaming about earning lots of money. Not for the sake of the cash itself, but for the lifestyle it could bring. Being able to travel all over the place and to buy whatever you like, that's what appealed. Imagine if I'd known back then that, only ten years later, I'd find myself at an after-show party during the Cannes Film Festival. Not just any party, but one attended by Leonardo DiCaprio and Paris Hilton herself. I also saw loads of supermodels – I recognised lots of faces but I didn't know many names. Paris looked wonderful, just as I'd seen her on television, with her expensive diamond-studded lace dress and flawless hair and make-up. At first she stayed on the sofa, but before long she started dancing. I had had a few cocktails by this point and I felt I just had to say something to my childhood idol. So I went straight over to her and asked for a hug.

'Sure,' she smiled, and gave me a long, warm hug and then we toasted each other. Imagine if I had been able to tell that to the teenager with the thick glasses!

I used to watch all the teen dramas on TV and I would fantasise about what life would be like if I lived in America. Everything looked so exciting, so much fun, not to mention the undoubted bonus of the weather, at least in the locations where those shows tended to be shot.

I've always hated winter. Sure, I played in the snow as a kid – I built snowmen and made snow angels and went sledging with my sister, but then most children have an almost magical tolerance of cold – somehow they don't really seem to feel it. These days I can barely be outside for twenty minutes in winter without my face hurting, no matter how many layers I'm wearing. I'll start muttering about Siberia and freezing to death as soon as the temperature drops below zero. It is dark, cold and grey and the sun barely shows itself; it sucks the energy out of me. Quite simply, I am not built for winter.

Back then, everything boiled down to my wanting to be like Malin Baryard or Paris Hilton. When the time came to choose my subjects for high school, my careers adviser told me to pick something that looked like fun and I was into horses and dogs so I chose land management. Looking back, that might not have been such a well-thought-out move. Dreams of breeding lapdogs or entering show-jumping competitions while living the Paris Hilton lifestyle didn't really fit with the harsh reality of sitting in a classroom with twenty fifth-generation farmers and learning all there is to know about heifers, sows and arable patterns. So before too long I started to skive. Once you realise you can get away with it, and there's a whole world out there, one that just carries on while all the young people are stuck behind desks, it's hardly surprising that the big wide world becomes more appealing than the next lesson, the one about which illnesses affect cows that are not properly fed. With the benefit of hindsight, I should clearly have just changed schools, maybe studied business or marketing. My parents took their usual approach of letting me choose my own path, for better or worse. When I did eventually quit, after two years and with incomplete grades, they weren't exactly shocked.

Next came a period where I didn't do much at all: I spent most of my time at home watching telly. As soon as I was eighteen I started going to the only decent nightclub in town and, since I was neither working nor going to school, it was never very long between visits. Being out three or four times a week was pretty standard. My friend and I soon realised that we liked everything about going out. We drank, danced, flirted and lived a carefree life. Occasionally I would meet a fit, charming guy and then end up going home with him. I had a pretty carefree attitude to sex too. I'd lost my virginity at sixteen, at a house party, to a guy who was two years older than me and drop-dead gorgeous. I hadn't had that much to drink and I definitely wasn't drunk, yet my abiding memory of that first time is how much it hurt, even though he was very gentle. We saw each other a few times after that – the difference between our first time and our second was huge. Suddenly I understood what all the fuss was about and I realised that I liked sex – a lot. We kept seeing and texting each other for a while, but it soon emerged that he was already living with someone. This didn't hit me too hard, I was mostly pleased to have learned about this new, wonderful thing that was sex, and when my friend and I did hit the nightclub I would happily seek out a hot one-night stand. The more I helped myself to it, the more my self-confidence grew.

Of course, that lifestyle couldn't go on forever – I had to get myself a job. My very first paid employment was at a café in a shopping centre. I was given a rota that meant working evenings and weekends too, and I could feel the resentment beginning to fester. I really wanted to work day shifts while my friends were at school and to keep the evenings free so that we could go out together. My boss showed me how to do jacket potatoes, make sandwiches, how to work the till and what to do at opening and closing time ... and I didn't like it one little bit. Standing there, slaving away for hour after hour, busy with the most mundane chores, missing a load of social events ... Then when my wage slip arrived, it was peanuts. I gritted my teeth and carried on though. At least I had a job, and what else was I going to do? With my incomplete school certificate it wasn't as though employers were fighting over me. At that particular point, I had no desire whatsoever to go back to studying: the time wasn't right. I was tired of school, and before too long, I was tired of work. Just the thought of going to work would make my skin crawl and all the time the wider world was tugging at me. I wanted to get out there, I just hadn't quite worked out how to do it yet. Being employed made me feel like the boss's personal slave. This having someone in charge of you, telling you where to be and when, saying exactly what you should be doing at any given point … no, no and no again. I wanted to be my own woman, make my own choices. I became increasingly disinterested at work and of course that didn't go unnoticed. The customers, of course, couldn't tell – my pride would never let that happen – but behind the scenes, things were going from bad to worse. Yet I still didn't want to quit, I felt that I'd prefer to get sacked. In the end, of course, I did, which came as a huge relief. After that, I tried my hand at all sorts of odd jobs: cleaner, care worker, product demonstrator, but they all went the same way in the end.

All that time, it never even crossed my mind to work as – for example – a stripper, even though I was liberated, self-assured and loved sex. In my world, strippers were women who deserved sympathy. People forced to do what they do, either by someone else or by desperate circumstances; people with no other way of putting food on the table. There was no doubt that these women must have been abused as children and they were bound to be junkies or alcoholics.

*

When I was nineteen, I met a guy in a bar. I fell for him pretty much there and then and it was the start of a long-term relationship. He worked as a builder while I had my odd jobs, but all the time the wanderlust inside me was just getting stronger and stronger. Sitting around waiting for my partner to come home from work – no matter how sweet, handsome or good in bed he might be – was simply never going to be enough for me. I was getting restless and that led to more and more arguments. Eventually, after we'd been together for almost two years, he asked me what the hell was going on in my head and I gave it to him straight. I told him I couldn't stand just sitting around in Uddevalla any longer, that the world was calling out to me; I wanted to go travelling. To my delight he said that he'd love to come along. So that was that.

I was twenty-one when we decided to go to Australia. We'd checked it out and apparently it was possible for under-thirties to travel on something called a working holiday visa, which is valid for one year. That way you could combine holiday and employment, and that seemed to be exactly what we were looking for. Neither of us really had anything tying us to Sweden, so we packed a rucksack each and then we were off.

We left another Swedish autumn behind and arrived in Australia in what seemed like high summer. I've never experienced anything quite so enjoyable as boarding a plane and flying out of the 'Kingdom of Slush'. As soon as I climbed out onto the aircraft steps, I knew I'd made the right decision – I belonged in the heat. Yes, I was going to have to work to support myself, but somehow any old job felt okay, as long as I was doing it in a warm Australian breeze.

Before long though, we'd discovered that the kinds of jobs that might be offered to backpackers were really badly paid so we spent our days sunbathing, swimming and partying, living in cheap hostels and cooking for ourselves instead. We lived cheaply, just doing whatever it took to allow us to enjoy life as much as possible. And what a life! It really felt like all the muscles in your body relaxed and unwound as they felt the sun's rays or the warm, salty waters of the ocean. But we also knew that the money we had wasn't going to last forever, so we made sure we always had an ear to the ground, hoping to find work that might suit us.

There was a free backpackers' magazine, available at most of the hostels we stayed at. Amongst other things, it had lots of job adverts, and that's where for the first time I saw a gentlemen's club advertising for girls. It said that the job was a perfect opportunity for attractive, charming girls who wanted to earn really good money while still choosing what hours to work. The 'choosing your own hours' thing was almost more important to me than the 'really good money' bit. I had no problem living frugally, even if my dream financial future was something far more prosperous. This independence that the ad promised ... I was curious. I was also pretty surprised by how open the whole thing was. I mean – a backpackers' magazine? When I brought up the subject with other people, I was met with a far more relaxed attitude than the Swedish one I was used to, which made me think. Maybe I was going to have to re-evaluate some of the things I'd had drummed into me back in Sweden? After some consideration I called the number and was invited for an interview. The interview itself was a pretty quick one – the guy in charge asked me straight away when I could start and that was more or less that.

My boyfriend really didn't like it and he told me he was going to end it if I started working there. Our relationship had been on the rocks for a while and I've never reacted well to ultimatums. We'd already split once and then got back together, and this ended up being the nudge I needed to make me move on. Despite all my prejudices I decided, just like that, to go for it.

I was ready to give stripping a try.

Chapter Four

MONDAY

MARTIN TRENNEBORG: *If you look at the whole picture ... if you disregard that minor detail, if you will, the abduction – then I have treated her well. That's my assessment. Of course she's less than happy about having been spirited away, but you can imagine how it could have been so much worse, there could have been violence and I don't know ... rape and so on.*

INTERVIEWING OFFICER: *Hmmm.*

MARTIN TRENNEBORG: *But I didn't do any of that, erm ... Well, it's not like she starved in there or anything, in fact they were, you'd have to admit ... reasonable conditions. To be honest, I expect she was better treated in the time she spent there than I have been here, by you.*

EXCERPT FROM INTERVIEW WITH
MARTIN TRENNEBORG

I wake up when I hear the door – the one here in my room – slam shut quite forcefully. It takes me a while to realise where I am, before my memory returns to full capacity. And then it's like my heart is being scrunched up. Nellie growls and that's when I realise that Martin is standing there, watching me from across the room.

'I'm glad you've eaten,' he says and gestures towards the table.

I haul myself into a sitting position and stare over. There's a plate there, with the remains of a sandwich on it.

Have I eaten? When was that?

I must be visibly confused, because Martin says: 'That's not unusual. You might experience a few issues with your memory. When you've had a bit of flunitrazepam, you know. It's basically the same as Rohypnol, especially at high doses. It'll all become clearer over the next few days, you'll see.'

He sounds friendly and relaxed – as though what he's standing there telling me isn't the slightest bit strange.

Especially at high doses.

Those words send a shiver right through me. *Imagine if he'd killed me by mistake? Given me an overdose?* My mouth feels horribly dry. I don't say a word – what is there to say?

Martin crouches down and beckons Nellie over. That's when I notice that he's got a lead in his hand and my whole body goes cold. *Is he going to take her away? What is he planning to do with her?*

Nellie, who is a very timid dog, obviously doesn't like Martin and she backs away when he calls her name.

Martin sighs and takes a big step towards her.

'No, you *can't*!' And suddenly, I'm crying again. 'Nellie, come to Mummy. Come on, poppet' – my voice cracks as I try to beckon her over.

'Listen, I'm just going to take her out for a walk,' he says and grabs hold of Nellie. He clips the lead onto her collar and then puts her on the floor. I can see her shaking.

He's lying. He's going to kill her. Or just let her go. There's no way she'll survive on her own.

'Please …' I whisper.

He gives me a funny look, then leaves, dragging a very reluctant Nellie behind him.

Minutes pass, and I go so quiet that my own heartbeat sounds like a kettledrum in my ears. Time is passing very slowly, and with each passing second I become more and more convinced that he isn't coming back; that I've lost my beloved Nellie.

Nellie, my only source of strength and solace.

If he comes back without her, I will kill him with my bare hands, I will …

That thought is interrupted by the sound of the external door and I hold my breath.

Please, please, please.

As I see Nellie coming back into the bunker, relief washes over me like a huge wave and I can't hold back the tears.

'Poppet!'

Martin takes her off the lead. He then pulls a clingfilm-wrapped sandwich from his pocket.

53

'I'm off to work. It's 7am. I'll be back later.' He glances down at the notepad and pen he gave me yesterday. 'You haven't written anything?'

No, I haven't. What do you expect me to write?

Martin sighs, picks up the pad and then drops it in my lap. 'Right,' he says sternly. 'I must get going.'

I shake my head.

'I see. So, no food then?'

I make eye contact for the first time that day; I can tell he means it. Resigned, I sigh and pick up the pen. My hand shakes as I move it towards the paper. Nothing. What am I going to write? I have no appetite at all. I do realise that I'm going to have to eat something though – I need to try to keep myself alive, as best I can. I mustn't give up. If I'm going to fight or flee then I'm going to need some energy.

I start writing in scratchy letters that don't even look like my handwriting: wholemeal bread, butter, cheese, tomatoes, muesli, yoghurt, bananas, apples ...

Put things that will keep you feeling full. Healthy stuff. You can scarcely move in here and God knows when you might see the sun again.

The voice inside my head is a sadistic one, but it's talking sense: I need nutrients. Vitamins. If I'm going to resist, that is. And resist, I decide right there and then, is exactly what I'm going to do.

I add dog food and a chew bone to the list before handing over the notepad.

'Would you like something to read too?'

I mumble that I wouldn't mind a few books – I can see myself going mad if I spend all my time staring at the plasterboard.

Martin looks pleased with himself. 'I've got some at home you can have.' He turns to leave, but then stops. 'You know when people are wrongly convicted of things?'

I don't know what he means and so I look puzzled.

'You know, like smuggling drugs into Thailand, that sort of thing?'

I screw up my forehead and nod warily.

'Yeah. If someone puts drugs in their luggage without their knowledge and then they get caught and end up in prison even though they're innocent. You know?'

'Yes?' My voice sounds thin and weak.

'You can look at this that way. Imagine you've been wrongly convicted of something and you're going to have to do a few years inside, only in this bunker instead of prison. You won't be receiving any visitors of course, but this is still better.' He smiles as though he's expecting me to suddenly realise how lucky I actually am, but I can't bring myself to say a word. He shrugs and heads for the door.

'Couldn't you …' I say gently, which makes him stop. My voice cracks, so I try again. 'Couldn't you just let us go?'

He raises an eyebrow, as though my question is patently ridiculous. 'No, that's not the plan. *Nooo. Sorryyy.*'

He checks his watch and scratches the back of his head. 'I really do need to go to work now, back later. You will get used to it, you know. And if everything goes according to plan, at least you won't be *alone* here for very much longer.'

My heart sinks. *The other toilets ... The second room.*
He's planning to kidnap someone else.

*

If you've never been locked in anywhere, it's impossible to imagine just how slowly the hours drag by. Martin said he was going to work, so I guess it must be just before eight in the morning. He also said that he'd be back after work. Most people work eight hours. Let's say he comes back in nine. Nine hours. Isolated in a tiny, dark, soundproofed bunker with nothing whatsoever to do, Nellie as my only company and only conversation. It doesn't take long for the silence to start to feel like a living thing, forcing itself on us from every direction.

At first, I just stay sitting on the bed, almost paralysed as the loneliness creeps in under my skin. I'm still struggling to come to terms with the notion that this is actually happening. There's no clock in here, so I have no idea how much time has passed, but eventually Nellie wakes me from catatonia with her whimper. I slowly pick up the sandwich I got from Martin. He thinks that's supposed to keep both of us going all day. My chin trembles as I

56

peel away the plastic and Nellie looks at me with such anticipation that you'd think it was a kilogram of mince I was unwrapping.

'Poor thing, you're starving, aren't you?'

I tear off small bits of the sandwich and feed them to her. She hasn't had a proper feed for over twenty-four hours ... or even longer? I don't really have an appetite myself – I guess that the shock has sent me into some kind of survival mode where I don't have time to feel hungry. Nonetheless I pop a few bits of bread into my own mouth. It takes ages to chew, as if it was fresh dough rising and expanding inside my mouth, but I force myself to eat – I'm going to need all the strength I can get.

Once we've finished the sandwich and I've changed the water in Nellie's bowl, I do a lap inside the bunker, examining everything. I feel a bit safer because Martin said he was going to work. He won't be back for hours. I lift things up, open cupboards, and it strikes me that, as much as I am looking for possible escape routes, I am also on the hunt for something I can use as a weapon if I need to defend myself, or if the opportunity arises for me to try to flee. He's been very thorough, though. What if my attempted attack, with the screws, was my one and only chance? What if that was my only chance and I blew it? I do my best not to think like that and even squeeze under the bed to see if there's anything I might be able to use under there.

There isn't.

Then I remember seeing some planks in the smaller room. I peer through the doorway and study them. *And it looks like . . .*

My heart starts pounding even harder.

It looks like they've got nails sticking out of them. I step into the room.

Nellie, who's watching intently from my side, barks suddenly. It's almost scary sometimes how well she reads me, how in sync she is with my emotions. I pick her up and give her a kiss on the nose.

'Right, you sit here a minute.' I put her down on the bed. 'I'm going to get us out of here.'

I go back in and I can see the planks there in the gloom. They're really long, but it looks like they've got two nails at the bottom, two in the middle and two at the top. I grab hold of one, but the weight of it coming towards me almost knocks me off my feet. I place them as carefully as possible on the floor. What if it leaves tracks in the dust? What if he sees that I've been rooting around in here?

I instinctively draw my arms to my chest and listen for footsteps. None arrive.

You mustn't forget to put them back exactly as they were, once you're finished, says the little voice accompanying me, my new sidekick. Wise.

Hope flickers into life when I see that, sure enough, there are nails at both ends and in the middle. I give them a tug, try to pull them out. They're stuck, but not hammered all the way in. I start waggling, back and forth, carefully at first and then progressively harder. Pretty much immediately, my fingers start hurting and I'm getting marks on my hands. What if Martin sees cuts on my hands when he gets back? He might realise that I've been doing things I shouldn't have.

My jaw is creaking – that's how hard I'm clenching – but the nails won't budge. That's when I have an idea: there was a tea towel on the worktop earlier. I jump to my feet and all my joints crack. Now, with the tea towel in my hands, I have another go at pulling out the nails. Careful! He mustn't find out what I've been up to.

Back and forth . . . My fingertips are screaming out in pain. Back and forth . . . I become completely obsessed with getting those nails out. It's all down to me, this is something I am in complete control of. And I'm not about to give up, even though it feels like my fingers are burning. The desperation fuels me onwards.

When one of the nails finally gives way and comes loose, the tears start rolling again. I look around. Where am I going to hide them? It seems silly not to have them close at hand, but I've no way of knowing whether he's going to go through all my clothes or not. The nails aren't particularly long, maybe five centimetres, yet it still feels reassuring to have them in my pocket. As I bend down to pick up the plank, there's a stabbing pain in my thigh.

'Idiot,' I mutter to myself and try to adjust the nails in my pocket so that I won't hurt myself with them.

Now I just hope that Martin doesn't find out what I've done. Just that thought brings the adrenaline rushing back. I look at the plank and think it looks obvious, that anyone can see there are two nails missing. I carefully put it back where it was, with the empty holes at the bottom. My heart skips a beat. *Is he going to notice?*

I take one of the nails out of my pocket and hold it up in the stark light of the bulkhead lamp. It might not be very long, but it certainly looks sharp. I try different ways of holding it in my hand and visualise sinking it into the eye or the carotid artery of the psychopath who's locked me in here. Which grip gives best purchase?

Is it even possible to hurt somebody with something this small?

I'm filled with doubt. If it comes down to a real fight, if it's me or him, then of course I want to cause as much damage as possible. Losing his sight would be a major injury, but it won't kill him so the carotid artery is a safer bet.

Where is it, though?

The ridiculousness of the whole situation doesn't strike me even when I stand in front of a little mirror hanging on the wall in the toilet section of the bunker. Everything else might seem unreal, bizarre even, but this – actually getting hold of a weapon and working out how best to use it against this monster – feels so right. I look at myself in the mirror, ignoring the smeared make-up and the rashes and spots I'm getting from the dry, dirty air in here. I pull my hair away from my neck and start feeling with the nail. Is that the carotid artery? That? There maybe? I practise on myself and try to memorise where the artery is, my determination increasing with every passing second.

If it does come down to it, I will kill him.

The last thing I do is check my neck to make sure I haven't left any marks, then I put the nails back in my pocket. I try to keep them horizontal so that I don't stab myself as I move. It really doesn't look like much, but somehow it makes me feel better – knowing I've got them and having visualised how I could use them to kill Martin Trenneborg.

What will he do to you if you try, but fail?

I straighten up with a jolt, almost as if it was a real voice talking to me. Then, out of nowhere, my thoughts turn to Mum. And my sister. I wonder what they're doing right now. Whether they've even noticed that I'm missing, or perhaps they're just going about their lives as normal, smiling and wondering what to have for dinner? Sis might be playing with her kids, laughing away till she's red in the face. Maybe she's kicking a ball around with her boys?

And I'm stuck in here.

I don't know how many tears the human body can hold, but at this point I discover my own reservoir is far from drained.

*

The hours, somehow, have passed. I didn't sleep much at all last night and I know I'm exhausted, yet each time

I've lain down to try to get some sleep, the thoughts, the fear and the bottomless despair have kept me awake. I've paced up and down in the tiny space available. Seven steps, then I have to turn around and come back again. I did try counting steps for a while, but I soon lost count. I've also tried hundreds of combinations on the code lock. Even though I know it's a waste of time, I can't help myself. Clicking frantically, to no avail. I've lost track of the number of times I've gone through every square inch of the bunker, looking for some way out. Every time it ends with my bursting into tears. I am being held captive and there really is no way out. The only person who can let me go is the person who put me here. The powerlessness is like a straitjacket, one that wraps me up so tightly that I can't move. The only thing that keeps me going is Nellie and thinking about my friends and family; thinking about the future that I had been looking forward to. It's really hard, I notice, not to give up – it's like there are long claws grabbing at me, voices telling me I haven't got a hope. That there's nothing I can do.

I *must* refuse to believe it.

Finally I hear the doors again and, despite the complete silence that has dominated for so long, it is not a welcome sound. It takes its toll – hour after hour after hour of silence, loneliness, isolation … The noise of the psychopath approaching though is worse still. I climb onto the bed and sit at the head end, Nellie in my arms. As the innermost door swings open, I hear Martin grunting and the sound of something scraping along the floor.

What is it he's brought with him?

I still haven't managed to work out *why* he's brought me here. What is it he's planning to do with me 'for a couple of years or so'? Everything I can think of, having heard tales of similar scenarios from around the world, is dreadful. Other men who have kidnapped women and held them captive have gone on to rape and assault them; tortured them for their own sick pleasure. In some cases they have even fathered children who have also been raised in captivity and many of the women have been murdered. Try as I might, I can't shake those thoughts. It's like a constant whining in my ear, like tinnitus with a persistent evil message. The fear is relentless and exhausting.

Martin finally enters my part of the bunker. He's brought a fridge and he's pushing it along on a little trolley. Seeing how pleased with himself he appears to be makes me want to scream.

If he asks me how my day's been, I'm going to throw up.

But he doesn't. He positions the fridge between the doorway and the table. When he glances over towards the other room, my heart stops beating for an instant. *This is it. Is the plank exactly where it was before? Is he going to notice that I've taken the screws out? What would the punishment for that be? He's already told me that if I try to escape he'll chain me to the bed; feed me bread and water. Maybe he'll punish me some other way.* The thought of being not just locked in here, but also chained to the bed so that I can't move sends a great shiver down my spine.

He bends down and starts fiddling with something on the back of the fridge. If he just moves slightly to the left then he's going to have a head-on view of the plank that I put back; of the empty holes where the nails were.

I hold my breath.

But he just plugs the fridge into a socket and then straightens his back.

'Right.'

That's all he says. He inspects something on the back one more time before heading back to the doorway to collect something else: two bags, one of which is making a chinking sound. I try to rein in my imagination. He lifts one of the bags onto the table and then proceeds to pull out its contents: it's the food I wrote down in that list. I get a pang in my stomach when I spot the cheese and tomatoes and I realise my body is hungry, even if I haven't really noticed. Even Nellie, who has consistently given Martin a wide berth, cautiously pads over, stands at his feet and then peers up at him with her innocent brown eyes as he pulls out a bag of dog food and a chew bone. He bends down and gives her a little pat.

'Yes, doggy. I'll give you some food now – we're just fattening you up for Christmas dinner.'

My whole body freezes.

As he says it, Martin gives me a look and a little snigger before he carries on emptying the shopping bag. *What was that snigger supposed to mean? That he was joking? That he wants to make sure I know who's in charge?* I start to feel dizzy, almost faint. I strain every muscle in my body. Nellie throws herself at the food he has scooped into a bowl. While she's eating, Martin carries on unpacking the other bag. It's a set containing a small frying pan and a saucepan; also a plate, cutlery, a drinking glass and a mug.

All of them look like weapons to me.

But then I remember what he said earlier – about having been an elite soldier and how I wouldn't have a hope against him. And then I play the scene in my head – me trying to attack this man with a mug, or a fork. It's just laughable and every scenario I invent ends with him fending off the attack and then punishing me. Or Nellie.

'That went well,' he says out of nowhere, which brings me back to earth. I must've disappeared into my own thoughts for a moment because he's unpacked everything and is now sitting on the chair next to the bed. I'm grateful that he isn't sitting on the bed itself – he seems to at least be keeping his distance. He nods towards the fridge in case I wasn't sure what he was talking about.

I look over at it, then at him again and say nothing. He sighs.

'How are you feeling today? Memory any better?'

I am struck by the thought that he's using the same tone with me that he would at work, when he's talking to patients. *How are you feeling today then?* I shudder. Doctor . . . a job that brings power over other human beings and one that involves huge responsibility. I bet his patients think he's kind and thoughtful, and they tell him their innermost secrets. Because you just have to trust your doctor. The thought that he might head down to his bunker to feed his captives as soon as he gets in from work is not something that would ever occur to any of us – it's just too absurd.

I tell him that I can't remember anything besides what he's told me and – apart from a few seconds when I came to in the car – that also happens to be the truth. Whatever happened between my eating those strawberries and waking up in here is one big black hole.

Martin nods slowly. 'I had planned to pack all your stuff away and tidy up after us. In your apartment, I mean.' His speech has slowed again and he seems a bit preoccupied.

I straighten myself up where I'm sitting. It's impossible not to be interested or want to hear more. However nauseous his voice makes me feel, he is the only one who can tell me what's happened to me. And who knows, maybe he'll let slip some tiny detail that might be useful to me. Hope, that warm, glowing ember, it's back.

'Okay?' I say weakly, hoping to encourage him to continue after he goes quiet.

'Yes, that's it. Clean, do the washing up, then lock up and throw the keys through the letterbox.' He snorts as though something funny has occurred to him. 'I'd been through various ways of getting you to come along, thought about knocking you out or threatening you at gunpoint. The best option though, clearly, was to spike you. But then, as I said, it took so much longer than I was expecting, so I didn't have time to tidy up. Obviously it doesn't look good – it's as if you've just disappeared. But I've got your keys and I'm going to go back on Wednesday or Thursday. I'll be able to bring some of your stuff down too. That'll be nice, won't it?'

He looks at me and I find myself nodding. That seems to be good enough for him and he goes on, more assured.

'Yes, I'll tidy up, chuck the keys through the letterbox and write a note to your landlord, saying that you've gone . . . somewhere. Of your own accord.'

My thoughts begin to race out of control. I really hope that I will have been reported missing by then; that they'll have realised I've been kidnapped and maybe the police will have my apartment under some sort of surveillance. They'll see him going into the building, then arrest him and force him to say where I am. That glowing ember inside me gets warmer and the light gets a little bit brighter. Wednesday or Thursday . . . By then, surely someone *must* have realised that something's wrong? My friend Nathalie, maybe. In the middle of last week we were talking about meeting up on Sunday. Sunday was yesterday. We hadn't actually arranged anything, no time or place as such, but she must've called and texted. Maybe she's tried to get hold of me on Facebook? You can see when someone last logged in and she knows I'm usually on there all the time. But now I haven't logged in since Saturday. Maybe she realises? And my friend, the policeman – we were supposed to meet early this week. They must be wondering why I haven't been in touch, or why I haven't been answering when they've tried to get hold of me. Surely they'll realise something's up? If I'm lucky, the police will be watching my apartment and they'll arrest Martin. If, on the other hand, *if* he comes back here ... If he does step through that damn door, carrying my bag with all my stuff in it – that will be the end of any hopes I might have about people finding out where I am. In which case I'll have to change my strategy. I won't be able to play along, no more cooperating or being nice. Then it'll be 'kill or be killed'.

Martin interrupts my thoughts: 'I've been looking at adverts for a while.' He adjusts his chair, so that he's sitting more comfortably. 'But until now I hadn't found anyone worthwhile.'

I feel sick, but I listen carefully.

'You, though, you looked great,' he says with a smile. 'And you seemed to have your head screwed on. A good, business-like profile, you know. Lots of the other escorts ... hmm ... most of them, in fact, seem neither sensible nor business-like and, to be perfectly honest, they're not even particularly attractive. And then of course you'd put that you were only going to be in Stockholm short term, so, yeah, I had to go for it.'

He laughs.

I wipe away the tear attempting to roll down my cheek.

'It was the strawberries, right?' The question just slips out.

Martin seems genuinely surprised that I'm actually talking to him and raises an eyebrow. 'Of course it was.'

'But,' and this part comes out as a whisper, 'you ate some yourself.'

He laughs again and seems to inflate himself in the chair. Proud.

'I'd marked them – a tiny black mark on the leaf at the top. You didn't see them. You wouldn't – no one expects that. You got the ones with the black marks. I ate the others. And then you drank the juice too.'

I get confused and try to sort my thoughts into some kind of order. The juice? I didn't drink any juice: we drank champagne. It must be written all over my face that I don't understand because now he leans in and props his elbows up against his knees as he explains, slowly: 'As I said, it took a bit longer than I'd bargained for. First, you fell asleep and I was down by the car, sorting a few bits and bobs, then I sat there thinking for ages and you sort of came round. I had a bottle of juice with me, spiked with flunitrazepam. It wasn't difficult to get you to drink it – you said you were absolutely parched.'

You shit!

I want to swear at him. At the same time, I'm thinking it's good he's telling me all this. I get the impression that he's telling the truth, even if he is still being very cautious. As though he doesn't want to give too much away about himself. That gives me some hope that he is actually planning to let me go someday, which is why he doesn't want to say too much. I realise that I need to be a bit careful about the type of questions I'm asking. If I get too personal, and he reveals his true identity, then he might decide to murder me instead. I start feeling dizzy again and I push the heels of my hands into my eyes.

'I'm sure you don't even remember us having sex,' he says with a giggle.

'Having sex? On Saturday? That wasn't what we'd agreed. We were going for dinner and then we were supposed to be coming back to my place.'

So he's had sex with me, on Saturday, when I was so drugged that I can't even remember. I want to say something about that being rape but not a sound crosses my lips.

'That's good, anyway,' Martin carries on, but I don't know what he means.

'Good?' I manage.

'Well, that you weren't completely unconscious. Easier to move you around that way.' He smiles. 'Down to the car. I had a wheelchair in the boot. I went and got it, and a few other things, while you were asleep. An intravenous pump. Yes – you have to keep the dose constant if you don't want the person you've sedated to wake up.'

'You could've killed me,' I whisper.

At this he looks a bit hurt – 'I am a doctor, you know. I know what doses to administer. And I had an antidote with me in case it turned out you couldn't take high doses. I was measuring your blood pressure throughout the journey.'

An intravenous pump. That explains the cannula in my arm when I first woke up; that was how he kept me unconscious for the whole trip.

'I'm going to bring your stuff down here. And then, if everything goes according to plan, there'll be another girl here. Or maybe several.'

This is almost too much for me to take in, as though I'm starring in some awful film.

'What do you mean?'

He goes quiet again for a while, as though he's weighing up how much to say. Then he seems to make up his mind that it's okay to tell me.

'Yes, another escort, I mean. Maybe a … a Brazilian girl. She lives in London. I can't get another one from Stockholm. No, no, that would arouse too much suspicion, if two escorts from Stockholm suddenly go missing.' He taps himself on the temple as if to say that yes, he's thought this through. 'This girl, though? No problem, I've already got the fake ID – you can get anything on the internet, you know. Not just escorts.'

He smacks his lips again. 'I'm going to invite her to Sweden. First, I'll go to Western Union wearing one of the masks and send her an advance to make her feel safe about the whole thing. Half maybe?' He pauses as though waiting for my opinion on the subject.

But I just shake my head. Nellie has finished her food and she jumps up onto the bed – I pull her close.

'Then we'll check into a hotel, me and her. She'll get some strawberries – well, you know how that bit works – then I'll put her in the wheelchair and check out. I'll say she's ill ... if anyone asks, that is. And then I'll bring her here.' He nods towards the room next door.

I try and imagine being here, with another woman in the room next door. My emotions go haywire.

'Or!' he suddenly exclaims, raising his index finger. 'Or I could bring a celebrity. Wouldn't that be something? Maybe ... hmm.' He drums his fingers against his bottom lip, naming famous Swedish singers as he does so. 'I could dress up as a plumber and knock on the door and say there's a problem with the pipes. Then I grab her. Wouldn't that be cool?'

He stops talking and looks at me like an expectant child, obviously wanting me to respond. But I don't know how I'm supposed to react. What's the right thing to say in a situation like this? How do you deal with a psychopath anyway? Should I play along or be difficult?

'Actually a celebrity would be a bit tricky,' Martin says after a while. 'They're probably all divas and that would just be a pain.' He wrinkles his nose.

If I'm diva-like and he thinks I'm a pain then maybe he'll let me go?

Or else he'll kill me.

Yes, that might just make everything worse. I do remember him opening up a bit, during our chat on Saturday, saying how hard he'd found it to meet women. How it was all down to the defect on his penis and that a lot of people have treated him badly. I don't want him to see those girls who've rejected him in me, and for him to take his frustration with women in general out on me. If I'm *not* like those girls were – if I'm kind and compassionate – then maybe he'll start to see me as something more than just an escort he found on the internet? He might start to like me, but then he mustn't get too fond of me. If this guy falls in love with me I've had it – that would give him yet more reason to keep me here for a couple of years perhaps, maybe forever.

I decide to continue with the friendly and accommodating approach, but still keeping pretty neutral so that he doesn't see me as a threat, or a thing. No, I want him to see me as a human being: as Isabel, a human who has dreams and plans for the future and people she loves. And who wants to go home ...

'No. No celebrities then, perhaps,' I say cautiously.

'Hmm.' He goes quiet, then lights up. 'Is your mum pretty? I could get her too.'

I hiccup and the tears start pouring, out of control. *Is he being serious?* It really is so draining, trying to keep up with Martin's mood swings; constantly trying to work out whether he's joking or not. I'm still no closer to understanding how he works and that in itself scares the shit out of me.

'No, she isn't,' I whisper as I dry my cheeks as best I can.

'Hmm,' is all he says. Then he slaps his knees, quite hard, which makes me jump. 'Right, how about it? Shall we go out?'

Out? Does he mean ...?

I don't know where it's been in the meantime, but he pulls out the lead that he took Nellie out with that morning. My heart sinks: he was talking to Nellie. But then he pulls out a pair of handcuffs and chucks them on to the bed.

'You too,' he says.

I stare at the metal hoops lying by my feet. My brain is racing and my heart is threatening to pound its way out of my chest. If I put them on, I'll be completely defenceless.

'Don't you want to go out?' Martin says, and the tone of his voice has changed, no longer relaxed. He sounds impatient.

I do want to go out. I do want to go out. I do want to go out.

After more than forty-eight hours in this dusty, dry, airless bunker, my body and soul are screaming out. I daren't quite believe it; I don't know what he means. *What are we going to do outside? Is this just a way to get me into the handcuffs so that he can do whatever he pleases with me?* I notice that I'm fiddling with the outside of my jeans pocket, feeling the outline of the nails through the denim. I force myself to stop to avoid drawing his attention to it.

'I … I …' I stutter, and I have to gasp for air and try again. 'I *do* want to go out.'

'Put them on then.'

I sniffle; dally for a second. But as Martin coaxes Nellie over and he puts her on the lead, I pick up the cuffs and hold my wrists out towards him. He clicks them shut around my wrists, first one, then the other. As they snap into place, a thought flashes through my brain.

I've signed my own death sentence.

I can feel the look I give Martin is a pleading one. Submissive. Imploring. And although I hate him so much for having done this to me, I realise it must be for the best that I don't let on.

'Come on,' he says and stands up.

The thoughts start racing again. *Where is it we're going? Are we really going out, outside of the bunker? What if I can get away?* At the very least, I need to memorise as much as I can; everything I see. If I get the chance to talk to anyone. So that I can explain what my surroundings look like, here, where I'm being held.

I feel my legs trembling as I get to my feet. With my hands cuffed, I stroke a lock of hair off my face. Then a nod that says I am ready. That says I do want to go out, and that I'm not about to cause him any trouble.

With him standing right in front of me, tapping in the code for the first door, I can't help but notice how my legs are twitching. He's covering the keypad with one hand so that I can't see the code and when the door finally swings open every fibre of my being wants to barge past him and just start running. Then I remember about the other two doors. And he's got Nellie, on her lead.

My throat is dry and I gulp as I pass through the first doorway — even that feels like a big deal, like entering a world you've heard so much about but you've never been able to visit. I try to memorise as many details as possible without it being obvious what I'm doing. Nellie, who of course has already been out with him, is straining at the lead: she knows the way.

It's not quite as light in here as it is in the bunker itself but we're standing in a pretty large space, that much I can see. Just outside the door there's a wheelchair and Martin sniggers and nods towards it; tells me that's the one he wheeled me around in. A shiver goes through me as we carry on walking. There's a bathtub over there. And a step-machine. A selection of dumbbells along one wall … So he's counting on me staying in shape while I'm here, is he? Those things might not even be for me. Maybe he's the one working out in here – it is outside my room, after all. The concrete floor in here is cold but the sensation of walking on new ground is powerful, almost overwhelming. We keep walking, past the bathtub and into a narrow passage. Martin tells me to go ahead of him, presumably to make sure he can keep an eye on me at all times. The whole place has that building site smell. There's no lighting in this part and after a couple of metres I can only sense him, like some evil spirit in the darkness. Then, finally, after what I'd guess was maybe ten metres, the corridor turns left again. I realise we've just walked round the outside of 'my room' – the wall to my right is also solid concrete. No wonder he says no one will hear me if I do try screaming.

Martin tells me to stop, right in front of a door. He walks past me, pulls out a bunch of keys and glances over his shoulder at me.

'Right, no funny business.'

I nod and give him my word – I desperately want to get through this door and then out on the other side.

When he does open the door, I'm actually a bit disappointed at first, because it's dark outside. Then the fresh air hits me. It's been raining. Martin has a torch and he leads the way, with Nellie behind him and me at the back. Carefully, ever so carefully, I put my foot down on the grass. *Is it grass? Yes, yes, it is.* It tickles and it's moist, and the tears start welling up straight away. I try to take in my surroundings: it's like a little yard, maybe three metres by seven, enclosed by a high fence. Looking up, I can make out a few trees. I can't hear anything – no people, no traffic, nothing. It's deathly silent out there and it smells like damp woodland.

I take another few steps. Martin is standing a little way away with Nellie, who is doing her business. The feeling of real, living soil under my feet, fresh air in my lungs and then this wonderful smell is an unbeatable combination: it smells like freedom.

'Please,' I say and take a step towards him. 'Can't you just let us go? I really want to be ... free. I want to go home.'

He sighs and cocks his head while Nellie scrabbles around in the grass.

'Nooo. Sooorrrryyy.'

God, I hate those words. Calm, but determined.

'When the other girls arrive, you'll be able to come out into the yard together, when the weather's nice. Cuffed and gagged, obviously. You'll be able to get some sun, get nice tans,' he goes on.

I lift my face towards the heavens and send up a little prayer. To God. To the Almighty. To the satellites orbiting out there in space. To anyone, anyone who wants to listen.

Here I am, rescue me.

After a few short minutes, Martin says it's time to go back in. But I don't want to – I want to at least feel the fresh air on my face just a little bit longer. But then he grabs my arm and gestures sternly towards the door.

The feeling as I cross the last threshold and step back into the bunker is one of the most dreadful, desolate sensations I've ever experienced. Martin instructs me to hold my hands up so that he can take the cuffs off. With heavy steps I make my way over to the bed, sit down and then stare blankly at the floor between my feet. Those words of Martin's keep repeating like a scratched record.

I'm planning to keep you here for a couple of years or so.

'I'm going to sleep at mine,' Martin says as he picks up the carrier bags that he brought the food and other stuff in.

I look up and apparently I look surprised, because he adds: 'Right. We are going to sleep together, later. You're going to be my girlfriend now. Cook us dinner. We're going to have sex. I'm going to do a few tests on you to make sure you're not carrying any STDs, after that we won't need protection. I want to have sex at least twice, three times a day.'

His tone is exactly the same as when he was talking about bringing a celebrity down here. Or my mum for that matter: matter-of-fact and cold. The feeling I have inside is like something breaking apart. *Girlfriend? You mean sex slave who's going to cook and clean and who you can hump two or three times a day, whenever you feel like it, and without any consideration whatsoever for what I do or do not want.*

'Are you really going to let me go, later? After ... a couple of years?'

He nods.

'How do I know you're not planning to kill me?'

'Well, you can never be sure,' he says, and my stomach ties itself into a tight knot. Then he shrugs, as if to say he was joking, and adds: 'If I'd wanted to hurt you, I would've done it by now, don't you think? I'm not planning to hit you. Or murder you. I want you to enjoy your time here. Cook for me, sleep with me, have sex with me, like a girlfriend. I don't want to hurt you.'

I really don't know what to think. It seems he's being straight right now and, so far at least, he hasn't hit me. But how can I be sure that he's not just suddenly going to turn violent? He is obviously a psychopath and he doesn't understand how much he has *already* hurt me. Who knows what he's capable of?

If I'd wanted to hurt you, I would've done it by now, don't you think?

I look around the walls, slowly.

'This woman who's going to be in the other room. Is she also going to be your ... girlfriend?'

Martin punches in the code and pushes the door ajar. 'She'll only have part of the room,' he snorts. 'The rest of it is going to be a torture dungeon.'

He walks away as the heavy door slams shut behind him.

***

So I was standing there one evening, clutching the handle of a bag full of new lingerie and sexy dresses. Ahead of me, the imposing doors to one of the largest, most exclusive strip clubs in Melbourne. And yes, my legs were trembling and my psyche was split down the middle. Back in Sweden, this would never have occurred to me – tracking down a strip club and then going to ask for a job. Here, though, it somehow just seemed a bit more normal. Considering I'd found the ad in a backpacker magazine, there must be plenty of young, good-looking girls out travelling who supplement their income this way.

I took a deep breath. It still wasn't too late to turn around and go home. *What if it really is as smutty and humiliating as I always imagined? Yeah. What if?* I forced myself to stay with that thought. What was going to happen if I got in there and it turned out that I absolutely hated it, or the other strippers, not to mention the customers? Well, in that case I could just get up and leave and never set foot in there again. And, since I was on the other side of the planet, no one back home in Sweden would need to be any the wiser. But then what if it wasn't like that at all? Imagine if it was a decent place, nice people and a place where, as well as all that, I could earn lots of money. Why not grab the opportunity? Admittedly there were butterflies. It was exciting. My sense of adventure had been well and truly awakened.

The whole place felt classy. Mood lighting, chandeliers, the red satin curtains with their gold braiding reminded me of hedonistic neighbourhoods in Paris and the famous Moulin Rouge. The club itself was spread across two floors, with three small dance floors on the bottom floor and a large one upstairs. It was packed. The woman who had interviewed me had obviously not been exaggerating when she told me that this was one of the most popular clubs in town. Despite the constant comings and goings, it still didn't feel claustrophobic at all. I guessed that the doormen outside were making sure they didn't let too many people in. There were doormen everywhere, not just outside. They circulated around the club, keeping an eye on the dance floors and bars, the stages and even the room used for private dances. It was a calm, orderly environment with a good atmosphere amongst both the guests and the girls.

So, about the girls ... When I saw and then got chatting to them, my prejudices about tattooed, crack-smoking single mothers collapsed straight away. Most of them were incredibly attractive and clean, and several were basically models, even if some of them had a few more curves than you'd see on an average H&M poster – no bad thing, if you ask me. Not only that, they were friendly, content and kind – kind to me, and kind to their guests. With hindsight I realise of course that a bad attitude wouldn't keep them in the job for long, just like any other service industry. If the customers don't like you, you'll be got rid of sooner or later. The girls I spoke to had neither addictions nor broken childhoods to bear. These were simply attractive young women who had found a way to earn lots of money.

After a while I found myself standing there alone and feeling a bit lost, when I suddenly saw a slim blonde with a beautiful face and a body to die for coming towards me.

'Hi. You must be Emma?'

Yes, I replied, that was me. No one uses their real name when they're working at a strip club, this much I had worked out. She introduced herself but I've forgotten her name. We'll call her 'Adrienne'. She moved gracefully, effortlessly and elegantly through the crowds; she showed me what was what and explained how everything worked.

You were expected to do a few dances on stage every night. Wearing lingerie. The performing on stage part was something that made me quite nervous to begin with. I'd convinced myself that you needed to be some sort of acrobat and perform all kinds of complicated moves on the poles, but in fact only a couple of girls were actually any good at that. They could hang upside down, spin around and fall into the splits and God knows what. The others danced more sensually, showing off their bodies. Not all of the stages even had poles. Adrienne gave me a few pointers and told me to watch the others a few times, that I'd soon pick it up. Besides, the onstage dancing wasn't the main event; that wasn't where you earned your money. At this club, the dancers paid a small sum to come to work each night – I think it was about forty dollars. When you weren't on stage, you were supposed to move around the club in a nice dress and try to sell private dances. The money you earned from that was yours to keep.

But, God, was I nervous the first time I was about to go out on stage! I had a mental image of everyone in the club suddenly standing watching me. The nerves died down after a couple of minutes though, when I realised that it really wasn't too bad after all. There were loads of stages and there were always several girls dancing at any one time, so fortunately all the attention wasn't focused on me. I had noted roughly how the other girls did the moves that Adrienne had shown me so I climbed onto the stage, showed off my body, started flirting with people from up there and then, before I knew it, it was over. That was when the real work started.

'Real work' sounds a bit silly, considering all the crap jobs I'd done before I went to Australia. You had to put on a sexy dress, move around among the guests and approach them to ask, 'Hi, would you like a dance?' Sometimes you'd chat for a while, but the rules were that you had to move on if they hadn't taken you up on the offer within a few minutes. The idea was to make room for the next girl. That never really ended up being a problem though. There was a good turnover, plenty of people – usually I just had to ask them in my Swedish accent, or tell them I was from Sweden, and then it was a done deal. Swedish things are somehow exotic in Australia, and just like the rest of the world, people have heard about 'the beautiful Swedish girls' and 'Swedish sin'. All in all, things kept moving and it never got boring. In fact, I was doing so many private dances that I barely had time for any breaks.

When it came to the private dances, guests could choose to pay for one, two or three songs. A single song cost around twenty Aussie dollars, while the price for three songs was about fifty bucks. If an average song lasted about five minutes, that means that the average hourly rate for the private dances was at least two hundred dollars. Of course you weren't dancing non-stop in the private booths, but still ... And that's before I've even got to the tips. I usually worked between eight in the evening and six in the morning – a ten-hour shift. After two or three nights, I'd already earned some proper money, and I'd made it doing something that I found enjoyable, easy and exciting. All in all, it meant that I could spend my days lounging on the beach.

If a guest agreed to a private dance, we would head upstairs. As well as the main dance floor, there was a room with individual open booths lining the walls. Anyone walking past could see right in and the doormen were constantly pacing the floor to make sure everything was in order. I've heard all sorts of rubbish about these private dances just being code for sex, but in all the places I've worked, I've never known anything like that to happen. It's always just been what people call a 'lap dance'. We never called it that because we didn't dance in the guests' laps. We used to say 'private dance', because that's exactly what it was: an intimate, sexy, sensual dance. It is performance, a show involving striptease – which was something we didn't do on the big stage.

The doormen never had much to do. In all the time I was there, I never had a single customer who didn't behave himself – they all followed the rules and not one was unpleasant or difficult in any way. Not *once*. If, by contrast, you're out in an ordinary nightclub, you're more likely to find men misbehaving than not. Now of course there were those occasions when you'd notice that a guest had had a bit too much to drink, particularly towards the end of the evening, but they always behaved themselves nonetheless. I guess that the constant presence of the security staff had a calming effect and the fact that the guests knew they'd be out on their ear at the first sign of any funny business.

There was another Swedish girl at the club and she was beautiful, with brown eyes and thick, dark, wavy hair. We got on well and started hanging out together in our free time. My boyfriend, who by this point had become my ex, had returned to Sweden, so the other Swedish girl and I spent our days sunbathing and swimming and our nights off partying or going to nightclubs. I was working anything from two to four nights a week at the club and I had more money than at any other time in my life. I was genuinely surprised. Surprised by how easy and – quite frankly – how much fun it was. By how friendly and helpful the other girls were. By how polite the customers were. By how much money you could make. And I was surprised by the fact that I was completely in control. No one was forcing me to be there. No one gave me a rota with fixed hours that I was expected to turn up for. I could show up whenever I felt like it, pay my forty bucks and get to work. If I felt like going home after an hour, I would; if I felt like staying till six in the morning, it was fine too. And if I didn't feel like coming in for a week, no one said anything. The same was true if I decided to work seven days on the trot.

I never saw stripping as a sustainable choice for my future, not for a moment. But for the time being, it was a fun, well-paid job, something I was going to do during my stay in Australia. An adventure that brought plenty of cash – money I could put to one side while I worked out what I was going to do with my life.

*

Eventually I had to return home to Sweden for the simple reason that my visa had expired. If it hadn't been for that, I would have liked to have stayed longer – maybe even for good.

Back in Sweden though, I found myself agonising about whether I was going to tell Mum about my job Down Under. I didn't feel like I'd done anything particularly dangerous or immoral, all I had actually done was danced. And I'd earned lots of money and had a great time while I was at it. I was, however, still convinced that Mum (along with everyone else) held the same kind of prejudices as I once held myself.

When I got home I had a lot of money and of course Mum wondered where it had come from. I've never been the type to go around lying or deceiving people. Besides, I love being able to be generous towards my family and friends, and it felt great to be able to give something back, especially as far as family was concerned. So I told her exactly what I'd been doing. Her reaction, it turned out, was fairly neutral: she wasn't exactly jumping for joy but then she wasn't fainting in disgust either. She could see that I'd made it home in one piece and that I was happy and excited – that was good enough for her. As usual, I was allowed to make my own decisions.

When I told one of my friends here in Sweden, she thought it was really cool. We'd be out, chatting to people, and she'd be bragging about it to them on my behalf. To be perfectly honest, I found that a bit difficult – I felt that I wanted to choose who I told myself. She just went round broadcasting it to all and sundry. Eventually I asked her to stop, she said she understood and promised to pack it in, but then, as soon as she got a few drinks inside her, the promise evaporated and she'd be telling everyone anyway. In the end, I couldn't really be bothered getting upset anymore. People's reactions were a surprise too. The majority were positive, thought it was exciting, or got a bit curious and started asking all sorts of questions. That wasn't really why I was going out, though – to be some kind of poster-girl for the stripping industry and have to tell everyone who was interested what it was like.

Going out was supposed to be about having fun!

Even though I'd brought a healthy bank balance back with me from Australia, I didn't want to just sit about kicking my heels and not doing anything. I'd decided I didn't just want to live off that money – I was going to save it. So after a while I started working in a strip club at home.

It was a very different experience from Australia, that's for sure. The clubs were smaller, not so exclusive; there weren't nearly as many girls or indeed guests. It could be ages before even a single customer turned up and then there'd be tough competition between the girls over who could 'get him'. Part of the problem was that it got very boring, just sitting there, waiting around, and the other thing was that there was much less camaraderie between us girls. Since the private dances were more expensive than they had been in Australia, it was still possible to earn a decent wage, but I definitely longed for the chance to work more, longed for that insane tempo and the great atmosphere at the club I'd left behind.

Back then, there were only three strip joints in Gothenburg and I worked in all of them. At one, competition between the girls was particularly strong and sharp elbows really were a must. I only lasted a couple of weeks there before I moved on to one of the city's other clubs. This one had a much nicer feel, the premises themselves were better and I quickly made friends with one of the other girls there. We used to go for a coffee or go shopping together, and sometimes we'd go out partying. It was great just being able to hang out with someone who not only knew what I did for a living, she also knew exactly what it was like. The way we could talk to each other felt really liberating. I'm pretty social in general – I find it easy to make friends and I do enjoy getting to know new people. The thing about moving around with work as much as I have is that new relationships often don't get the chance to develop as much as you'd like before it's time to up sticks and move on. Added to that was the problem of not being able to be completely straight about my occupation – I reckon over the years lots of potential friends or dates have noticed me hiding something. They might have found me reserved, when in fact I was just concentrating hard on not letting it slip.

One of the drawbacks with working in Sweden was the risk of being recognised all the time. I didn't want to shout my career choice from the rooftops, especially when people are always so keen to judge. Gothenburg is only an hour's drive from Uddevalla, so there were a few times when an old classmate, an acquaintance or maybe a friend of a friend turned up. Whenever they did, I would make a beeline for the changing rooms and ask the other girls to tell me when they'd gone. Usually there were so few people in the place that keeping track of them wasn't too difficult. It was busier at weekends, but again the clientele was different from Australia. Here, the customers were younger and most of the time they'd arrive after everywhere else had shut. As a result there was plenty of drunkenness and a fair bit of trouble. I used to drive to the club and I'd work from eight in the evening till five in the morning, two or three nights a week.

Even if she never said so, I always assumed my mum worried about me, so one day I actually invited her down to the club. She came in the daytime, before opening, and had a look round. She met my boss, realised it wasn't as edgy as she'd thought and then went home. As usual with Mum, that was the end of that. A lot of the time she would be getting up just as I was coming in, at half-six in the morning. That's when her day would start, while I'd be getting into bed. I tried to get eight hours most of the time so I'd be up just after two o'clock.

When I wasn't working, I used to hang out with friends: partying, shopping, walking, going to cafés or the cinema and, yes, there were a few dates too. Aside from the stripping, you could say that I had a pretty normal life for a twenty-something girl, even if I had a lot more disposable income than most of my friends.

Before too long, though, I started getting itchy feet again. Was this it? Was this what life was going to be like from now on? Living in Uddevalla, working in Gothenburg as a stripper, watching the days go by while I was just getting older, not really knowing what to do next? Increasingly, I felt that it wasn't the life for me. My inner adventurer was soon tugging away inside me. By the time autumn came round again and I found myself shivering in the car on my way to work, my mind was made up. There was nothing keeping me in Sweden and I needed to get out there and see the world again. Get away from those same boring old streets, those same old nightclubs, those same old people and the same old questions. What I needed was to spread my wings, take a leap out into the world and see where my spirit took me. Why not start in the country that I'd learned to regard as my second home? Once the idea had popped into my head, it was really only a matter of time. And when the first snowflake of the winter fell over Uddevalla, I was busy making arrangements.

I was going back to Australia!

Chapter Five

TUESDAY

INTERVIEWING OFFICER: *Do you know which day you took these blood samples from Isabel?*

MARTIN TRENNEBORG: *Monday, I think, must've been Monday. Possibly Tuesday.*

INTERVIEWING OFFICER: *Did she have to do all the tests in one go – both the blood and the smear?*

MARTIN TRENNEBORG: *All in one go.*

INTERVIEWING OFFICER: *All in one go.*

EXCERPT FROM POLICE INTERVIEW WITH
MARTIN TRENNEBORG

Last night was just like the night before. I've been tossing and turning in bed, unable to fall asleep, even though I can feel the exhaustion in every part of my body. Those words have been echoing around my head ever since he said them – I can't make them go away.

Torture dungeon.

Even if he hasn't hit me, or been violent – yet – I cannot stop thinking about it. Did he mean it, or was he joking? And the thing about Nellie ending up as Christmas dinner? I am so terrified that I'm shaking. I have to assume that someone who's capable of the things Martin has told me – like spending five years building a bunker, planning an abduction and then carrying it out – is completely devoid of empathy, which means that he's probably capable of doing just about anything to another human being. Who knows how a psychopath thinks, or what fantasies they might have besides locking a woman up and keeping her prisoner for several years?

I want to have sex at least twice, three times a day.

That look on his face while we were having sex on Thursday keeps popping into my head, and the way it makes me feel has me curl up into the foetal position. When the door finally opens and I realise it must be morning, I'm already wide awake. I've had an hour or two's sleep, at most. There's a horrible taste in my mouth and my hair is greasy and plastered to my scalp.

I sit up in bed.

'Good morning,' says Martin and mumbles something to Nellie too. I notice he's got his hands full of pharmaceuticals and a few other things. A toothbrush. He dumps it all on the table and picks up Nellie's lead. 'I'm taking the dog out. While I'm doing that, I want you to do those tests on yourself.' He nods towards them. 'I'm guessing you know how to do it?'

I do recognise the packaging: vaginal testing kits, to see if you've got chlamydia. I have used them a couple of times before. The relief I feel when he tells me I can do them myself makes me nod quickly several times.

'Yes, yes, I do.'

He puts Nellie on the lead. 'I thought so. But just to be clear: you put the cotton bud into your vagina and swipe it around a little bit, then you pop them into the little test tubes supplied.'

'Yes,' I respond.

'Then you'll need to do some blood tests too. I can do those though, once you've got these out of the way.'

He says nothing more and disappears off with Nellie. As I stare at the packets, I feel so completely humiliated, as though I don't even have a will of my own. No choice. And choice, I realise, is exactly what I've been deprived of. I remind myself of the plan: stay neutral, stay compliant. Then I shuffle my way over to the edge of the bed, open the packets and do the vaginal tests on myself. By the time I've done them, my heart is pounding so hard I can see it through the pink top, which by this point is pretty smelly.

He comes back just a few minutes later.

'Please,' I say. 'Can't I go outside for a little while? It would just be so nice to get some fresh air and see daylight.'

He looks at the little test tubes and seems pleased. Then he checks his watch. '*Noooo. Soooorryyy*,' he says. 'There won't be time for that today.'

I pluck up some more courage: 'Tomorrow? I would really like to get out for a while in the mornings as well.'

He gives it some thought. 'It'll be pretty early.'

As though I don't lie awake all night anyway.

'Oh, don't worry about that,' I say. 'It was so nice to get some fresh air.'

Martin replies that I will be allowed out this evening when he comes home from work and that tomorrow morning he'll take both me and the dog out. Getting permission to go outside, into a tiny yard with a patch of grass – being *taken out* with the dog – feels, in my twisted state, like a great victory. I thank him.

'Sit down on the bed.'

I obey him and watch as he opens a packet and pulls out a syringe. He takes hold of my arm and moves it towards the light.

'Hmm,' he says. 'Tiny veins. We'll have to use one of these.' He holds up some kind of large rubber band, then wraps it round my arm a few times before slapping lightly at the top of my forearm.

What if he gets it wrong?

I can feel myself getting nervous and my heart is racing.

I try to reassure myself with the fact that this man is a doctor and that he seems to know what he's doing. He jabs the syringe into my arm, but no luck – the blood just refuses to come. The pain though races up my arm like a flamethrower.

It occurs to me that in fact he *says* he's a doctor. Just as a few days ago, he *said* that he was a stockbroker. He might just as easily be a plumber or a caretaker. I can't trust anything he says.

He mutters, has another go and it hurts just as much this time around. He misses again, and again no blood appears. I'm starting to feel a bit dizzy and nauseous.

'I feel like ... I feel like I'm fainting,' I pant.

Martin sits up straight in his chair and looks me in the eye. His expression is so cool, so composed – completely heartless. I can feel my hands trembling again.

'Lie down.'

I obey, and immediately feel a bit better. Finally he has extracted enough blood and the procedure is complete.

'I'll take these to work with me and get them tested.'

Won't they be able to see that it's my blood? The thought occurs to me straight away but any hope it might give me is soon quashed by Martin saying: 'I'll put it in as unidentified – I'll tell them it's from an African refugee. There's no way it could be traced to you.'

I look down at my arm. 'Is this ... safe?'

He scoffs. 'You mean hygiene wise? You should've seen some of the places I've worked in with the Red Cross.' He laughs as though what he's just said is extremely humorous, but there's clearly a thinly veiled element of irritation behind it all. As though it's wrong of me to query what he's doing.

I clutch my arm and keep quiet – I daren't say any more on the subject.

'You've got some stuff there – toothbrush, toothpaste and so on. It's important that you look after your teeth, because you won't be getting any dental care here.' He pulls a little notepad from his pocket. 'Is there anything else you'd like? Toiletries, that kind of thing? Are you on any medication?'

I tell him I'm on the pill. When I realise that I haven't seen daylight for three days and I've no idea when I might next see it, I ask for vitamin D and Omega 3 supplements too. Martin nods and jots it down.

'Hmm. Do you use tampons or sanitary towels?'

'I ... I ...' It's so hard to carry on. This is such an intimate subject and I'm sitting here discussing it with a man who has kidnapped me. Eventually I do manage to find my voice again, even if it is weak. 'I don't usually get periods. The pill ...'

He hums again.

After a short while he stands up again. 'Right, you've got enough food to see you through. I'll be back straight after work.'

He stands there, as if waiting for me to say something. Biting his bottom lip. I still don't say anything.

'Yes. Goodbye.'

'Goodbye,' I respond and I force myself to make eye contact with him before he leaves.

To see you through, he said. Something about that bothers me, but I can't quite put my finger on it. I get to my feet, stop, then plod over to the door and put my ear to it. He said he was going to drive to work. My whole body strains and I hold my breath to see whether I can hear the car pulling off. If I can, there's a chance that I could make such a racket in here that someone else might hear.

To see you through. I frown. Then, for several minutes, I hear nothing. I feel the disappointment straining against my ribcage. Eventually I haul myself over to the fridge to get something to eat. The fact that I almost passed out when he was taking blood is hardly surprising – I've been this man's prisoner for three days and all I've managed to eat is a few strawberries and a couple of sandwiches. I've hardly slept and I've been drugged. This is not good. If I'm going to stand any chance of getting through this and then trying to flee, I'm going to need to be fighting fit. I decide to start working out while I'm in here, but not so much that it leaves me aching or makes me weaker. I also think about making sure I eat at the right times – I don't want to end up getting hungry too early.

To get yourself through.

As I put the butter back in the fridge, that's when the thought strikes me.

What if I don't?

I really didn't think I could be any more scared, but now something has occurred to me that makes the terror burrow even deeper into my soul: what if something happens while he's out? There's no way for me to raise an alarm and no way for me to get out either. If Nellie were to knock the lamp over and start a fire, or if something short circuits, then he's going to come home from work and find me burned to death. If he has a crash and ends up in hospital, or dies, then Nellie and I are going to slowly starve to death in here.

I hold back the tears and take a bite of my sandwich. Then I peer over at the lamp, which is very hot. I try to focus on working out. Planking exercises would work in here. And press-ups and crunches. Squats and thrusts. Running on the spot. Once I've got some food in me, I'm going to start working out.

And it's while I'm planking on the cold, dusty concrete floor that I suddenly hear something. A completely new sound. I hold my breath. It's a sort of murmur. Almost like ... voices? Like several people shouting, but from some distance away – through thick concrete walls.

For a couple of seconds I'm completely paralysed. Then I realise that it could be someone looking for me. Someone who has managed to track me down somehow, something Martin didn't think of. Or else it could just be people talking very loudly. Outside. But if I can hear them, they can hear me! My whole body suddenly fills with adrenaline and joy.

I climb off the floor and position myself underneath the ventilation duct. I have a look around, grab a saucepan. I slam it as hard as I can against the pipe. This brings a shower of dust that makes me cough but I still fill my lungs and roar for all I'm worth.

'Hello! Can anyone hear me?'

I scream louder than I ever have in my life.

'Hello! Help! I'm being held in here. Call the police!'

I can still hear the murmur. Nellie, clearly terrified, is cowering in a corner and staring straight at me. I've never seen her eyes so big, but for once I'm not thinking about her: this could be our chance. My heart is racing at a hundred and ninety and my cheeks feel warm. I jump down from the bed and run over to the door, and then start banging on that too.

'Hello! I've been kidnapped! Help me!'

I bang on one wall. On the pipe again. Then another wall.

'Please! Help!'

By now I'm so hoarse that I simply can't scream anymore, so I stand there, in absolute silence, and listen. I've exerted myself so much that my lungs are sore. *Is that something? A sign they've heard me? Maybe they're banging back?*

The murmur, though, is constant, as before.

I force myself to take a few deep breaths and to focus completely. *Are they really voices?* Silently I head over to where the sound seems to be coming from. Towards the table. *Are they on the other side of the building? No, it's ...*

Then there's a clunking noise inside the bunker and the sound disappears. The disappointment brought on by the hope and the joy I've just felt being quashed is the worst yet. There were no people. No distant murmur of voices. It was the fridge, just the compressor working away. The tears well up and spill over, and I collapse in a heap on the floor.

After a little while comes another clunk and the noise comes back. I drop the saucepan, which I've been holding in a vice-like grip, and the tears flow even faster.

Please, God, you have to save me.

*

When Martin gets home from work that day, I can tell straight away that something's not right. I can't quite put my finger on it, but as soon as he walks through the door I can see that he's behaving differently. Moving differently. Looks determined, but somehow ... distressed. The first thing that occurs to me is that maybe someone has found out where I am and that's why he's so stressed. He lets the door slam shut behind him and then he just stands there, staring at me. There's something in his eyes that wasn't there before, a real darkness, and yet again I'm gripped with fear. *I need to calm him down*, I think to myself, *whatever it is that's upset him.*

'Hi ...' I attempt softly, and I start standing up from the bed where I've spent the last few hours just sitting with Nellie in my lap, praying for God to help us. When Martin notices that I'm about to move, he pulls something from his belt.

'Sit down.'

I can't believe my eyes. I blink rapidly. Then I can see that it really is a pistol he's holding and my breathing cuts out. I sit there, as still as I can while clutching Nelly with a vice-like grip. She stares straight at Martin and her whole body is trembling. Whimpering. As though she can feel the threat in the air too.

So this is how it ends then? Is he going to shoot me and then bury me out here in the woods?

The tears continue, with renewed force, and I sense a flash behind my eyes. I take a deep breath as I prepare to do the very last, most desperate act a person can do: pray to God for mercy, to be spared. Images of my mum, my sister, my friends appear in my mind's eye. The horse I used to own ... Nellie ... Then my favourite childhood teddy pops into my head: white with a pink nose, claws and hair. I really did love that bear. I realise this is my life flashing before my eyes. It might not look like much, but it's *my* life and I don't want it to end with my being shot here, by this psychopath, in a shitty bunker, God knows where. No one will ever find out what happened to me and that in itself is a crushingly sad thing to deal with.

I just don't want to die.

And as the panic is about to take hold of me completely, Martin walks over and sits down next to me on the bed. Every muscle in my body is straining and I can't manage a word. He has the pistol in his right hand, resting on his knee, and for a long time he doesn't take his eyes off it. I can hear my own pulse in the silence. Eventually he looks up at me.

'I've been sitting with this in my mouth ... again,' then wipes the index finger of his left hand under both eyes. *Is he crying? I daren't look. No, no tears. His eyes are bloodshot though.* 'Must've done it fifty times. But I can't bring myself to pull the trigger.'

I listen, and try to understand what he's saying. *Does he want to kill himself? Shoot himself in the head?*

If he does decide to do that then I'm going to starve to death in here.

The thought fills me with fear. I have to say something. *Do* something. However fucked up it may sound, I need Martin Trenneborg to stay alive. He is my only chance of ever seeing daylight again. A cold sweat grips hold of me.

Then, though, he puts the pistol to one side and my heartbeat calms down a notch. It's lying there on the bed, between us. It seems to me to be radiating evil.

'Pick it up,' he says. 'Just shoot me. If that's what you want.'

My whole body starts shaking.

'Look,' he carries on. 'It *is* loaded.' He thrusts it into my hands and I have to stifle a scream. 'Just pull the trigger.'

The weapon feels hard, cold, in my hands. I handle it extremely carefully, terrified it might just suddenly go off.

'Just pull it, then it goes bang.' He's staring me straight in the eye and that fixed, cold look has returned; he looks like himself again. 'The doors are open. All you have to do is shoot me and walk away.'

I look at him, then the weapon and then close my eyes. *I can't. I cannot kill another human being, not even this one.* And to see it happen, to know that it was me that had done it, would be something I'd have to live with for the rest of my life.

Rest of my life? And how long might that be if I shoot him?

Oh yeah. Even if I do kill him, I still can't get out. He's the only one with the codes to the doors. I daren't take his word for it that they're open.

'I … I can't do it,' I whisper, still hoarse from all the screaming. But it isn't just the fact that I'd still be stuck. I discover, right there, that I simply cannot murder another human being. The nightmares would never end.

Martin stares at me, a long, inquisitive stare that gets right under my skin. Then he takes the pistol from my hands. I still don't feel relief, not yet – I don't dare. If I can't do it, maybe he can. Either right here, in front of me, or later on, at home. *What if he shoots himself tonight? Then I'll really be stuck. Abandoned. Doomed.* I need to say something. *Do* something. I force myself to put my hand on his thigh; squeeze it gently.

'You don't need to die,' I say as gently as I can manage, trying to avoid thinking about how absurd it is for me to be sitting here, trying to comfort my captor. 'Everything will … work out. Everything.'

He frowns. Then he gets up and walks out of the bunker, leaving me alone again, without another word.

For several minutes I sit there on the bed, completely silent and still. I stare up at the metal ceiling, half-expecting to hear a muffled gunshot while the hopelessness kneads my stomach. But it never comes. After maybe half an hour I hear the doors again and I purse my lips, terrified he might still have the gun with him, that he might have changed his mind.

105

Scared that perhaps he's got it with him and he's about to shoot me. But he hasn't.

He steps into the bunker carrying a large black plastic tray. I don't dare say a word – I just stare at him as he puts the tray down on the floor. It must be for Nellie, I realise. 'She needs to learn to go in this, otherwise I'm going to have to get rid of her,' he announces calmly. Then he adds something that I can't make out. I am just so incredibly tired, tired to my bones and down in the depths of my soul. Keeping up with Martin's mood swings and never really knowing what to expect is so strenuous. I'm constantly reminded that I am entirely at the mercy of this man. Nellie looks surprised, briefly inspects the tray but then hops out again and back up into my lap. I swallow hard. She has peed on the floor a few times, but I've been very careful to rinse with water and then dry it up so that it can't be seen or smelled – I don't want Martin getting angry with her. God knows what he might do then.

We're fattening you up for Christmas dinner . . .

There is a mat inside the tray too. Martin picks it up and then places it under Nellie's feeding and drinking bowls while muttering about what a terrible mess she's made. This is just so insane. Only a short while ago he was sitting next to me, holding a loaded weapon and asking me to shoot him. Now he walks in carrying armfuls of stuff for my dog and acts as if nothing has happened. I look over at my little Nellie, I feel so grateful she's here. Martin could just as easily have left her in the apartment when he kidnapped me. She would probably have starved to death, and even the thought of that is so terribly painful. But now she's here, unharmed, despite everything, and that gives me strength. It motivates me; it keeps me focused on getting out of here. I cannot let anything happen to her. As she snuggles up next to me in the bed, I notice her coat is full of dust and dirt. That gives me an opening, a way to break the awkward silence after everything that's just happened.

'Thanks for the tray,' I say as I stroke Nellie's back.

Martin stops what he's doing and looks at me with a frown. Then he lifts his head.

'You're welcome.'

'She's starting to get very ... messy. It's a bit dusty and stuff in here. She could really do with a shower.'

He rubs his chin with his forefinger and thumb, as though tugging at an invisible beard. 'I can bring a tub down that she can have a bath in every now and then.'

'But then she'll be bathing in all that dirt.'

Martin gives me an irritated sigh. 'It won't do her any harm. That's the way people used to do it. I'll be back soon, I'm just getting some more stuff.'

Once the door swings shut, I lift Nellie up, push my face into her coat and kiss her softly on the neck.

'I'm going to get us out of here. Somehow or other I'm going to do it,' I whisper.

When Martin comes back he's carrying a few tools, some lighting tubes and a dark-blue nightlight. He's also brought a clock radio. That does lift my spirits a bit. One of the things about being locked up for long periods of time without any contact with the outside world is how hard it is to keep any track of time. Now, although that might sound trivial, you actually realise after a while that it really isn't. Not knowing whether it's the middle of the night, early morning or late afternoon is distressing in itself, as is always having to ask.

'Books,' he says, and throws three of them onto the bed. I pick them up. One is *Smuts* by Katarina Wennstam, a thriller about buying sex. The next one is *Friend of the Devil*, a novel depicting the rape and murder of a woman. My stomach turns. *This hasn't happened by chance, has it?* I put it down and pick up the last one, *The Poet*, and read the blurb.

'Christmas presents, from years ago. I haven't read them though,' Martin tells me as he sorts through the tools.

The blurb on the third book very nearly has me in tears, but I hold them back as best I can. Now I know for sure that these books haven't been chosen at random, but are in fact – just like everything else – part of the wicked game that Martin is playing with me. *The Poet* tells the story of a serial killer who forces his victims to leave fake suicide notes before killing them.

You're going to give me your password. Facebook, email and so on.

Is that his plan? Make me write to family and friends telling them everything's okay?

It might be better for them not to know anything at all.

Instinctively, I try to banish that thought, but then I start to think that perhaps the dark voice inside me is right: for their sakes. The thought of my spending years in here and my family never finding out the truth ... They would never find peace. I realise what it means, my thinking like this, and I feel sick. I mustn't lose my grip, mustn't buy into this psychopath's way of thinking. I clear my throat.

'Listen ...'

Martin, who's busy with the fluorescent tubes, stops mid-movement. He's holding one of them up towards a little junction box on the ceiling.

'You said you were going to Stockholm ... tomorrow?'

He nods. 'Maybe. Maybe Thursday.'

'Can't we come with you?' Despite my having asked him to release us countless times, and having received the same response each time, it's just impossible not to ask again. 'I ... want to go home. I won't say anything, to anyone, I promise. I won't go to the police. I just ... I can't stay locked up in here for years. I just *can't*.' My voice cracks.

Martin sighs, shakes his head. 'I'll bring all your stuff. You'll be much happier here once you've got your things, just you wait.'

I chew on my bottom lip as I digest what he's saying.

'Do you have any suggestions? I mean, erm ... how to finish this place off? Now's your chance. You're going to be here for a really long time. You'll see. I'm going to sort out a telly. And a sofa, a coffee table, like a living room ... You can have an iPad too. No internet, obviously, but you can read books on it, or play games. Then, once I've got another girl in here, she'll keep you company. Won't that be nice? I mean, a bit of company, besides the dog? So … now's the time if you've got any requests for in here.'

I take a deep breath and my head slumps to my chest. 'No, I don't.'

Because I'm not staying here for long.

Martin shrugs. 'Do me a favour and pass me the drill?'

I look at all the stuff lying strewn across the floor and thoughts of hurting him and fleeing fly through my mind. *With what? The fluorescent tube? A nail? The drill?*

And as if reading my thoughts, Martin says: 'You still wouldn't be able to get out. You'd be stuck in here with a stinking corpse instead.'

He's right. If it does come to that, if I decide to fight for my life, my freedom, I'm going to have to do it when he 'walks' me.

*

After installing two fluorescent lights, plugging in a little lamp and putting the blue nightlight next to the bed, he sits down on the chair next to the bed and looks at me. He scrapes the dirt from under his fingernails.

'Is there anything else you want?'

I think about it. 'The Bible,' I say, after a long pause.

Martin raises an eyebrow and a mocking sneer spreads across his face. 'Seriously?'

I nod.

'Do you believe in God?'

I nod again. Because yes, I think I do.

'Hmm.' He leans back and crosses his arms as though that's the weirdest thing he's heard in a long time. 'I stopped believing in God,' he says after a while. 'I had this friend ... and he gassed himself with his own exhaust pipe. No one had suspected a thing, everyone thought he was doing fine. Then, one day, bang! Gone. God ...' He sniggers. '... I don't think so.'

If people stopped believing in God just because terrible things happen then I should've stopped long ago. I haven't, though – I pray, every day. Intently. Pray to God to give me another chance. I have, of course, wondered if this ... all of it ... is my punishment for the way I've lived my life.

'I would still really like to have it,' I blurt out.

'Yeah, yeah, I'll get you one,' he replies in a tone that says roughly: *Jeez, there are some weirdos around.* And once again I can't get over just how far gone this guy is – he thinks *I'm* the weirdo.

'I would also really like some ... you know. Underwear. Well, knickers at least ...' The humiliation sears across my chest.

He sucks his lips and nods. 'How long have you gone without a shower?'

Far too long. My hair stinks, so do my armpits. Not to mention down there. I've been wearing the same jeans, with no knickers underneath, since Saturday, and even though I have tried to wash myself in the little hand basin it hasn't really helped. I've had some unpleasant discharge and I think

I might have thrush. My hair is dry and greasy at the same time and I'm coming out in a rash. Not only that, I've got diarrhoea. The thought of a shower now, with hot water and soap, shampoo and conditioner, sounds like absolute heaven.

'Three days, I think.'

He gestures towards the shower in the other room. 'There's no hot water in here yet. Hmm … Right, you can come to my place to wash. Tomorrow. But after that, I'll make sure I hurry up and get this shower plumbed in so that you can use this one instead.'

At this point I feel that warm, red glow being fanned in my chest again. But I've been here before. Hope has been awakened then extinguished, time after time after time. It's exhausting.

'I … I would really like that.'

'But!' He gives me a stern look. 'Don't get any ideas. No smashing glasses, trying to escape or anything. Obviously.'

'No, of course,' I blurt out as fast as I can, even though it was actually my first thought. I wonder what his house is like, whether it would be easy to escape from. *Maybe there's a neighbour to run to?*

And what about Nellie? He's hardly going to bring her to the shower. And if I get away, she'll be left behind. I can't do it. Then what would he do to her? But then another thought starts crystallising at the back of my mind. I despise it; I do whatever I can to get rid of it, but can't.

If a chance to escape presents itself, I MUST take it. I can't stay here, in this psychopath's clutches, just for the dog's sake.

'How about sharing a bed tomorrow?' Martin's facial expression is completely transformed yet again. Now he seems euphoric. Dramatic mood swings, as ever.

Well, what the hell am I supposed to say to that? *Of course I don't want to sleep with you.*

'Yes ... we could do,' I reply, terrified of what might happen if I refuse.

He looks satisfied. 'Right, I'm going to mine to cook something. I'll bring you some when it's ready. Sound okay?'

I nod, even though I'm pretty convinced nothing is ever going to be okay again.

*

The next time I hear footsteps, I'm sitting on the bed. I assume it's Martin bringing me some food and, even though I'm not hungry, I realise that I do need to eat. I sit up straight. Only one door to go ...

A man comes in – a man with dark hair and a beard. A man who isn't Martin! Hot flushes alternate with wave upon wave of cold sweats. *What's going on? Who is this? Is he going to rescue me?*

The man just stands there. There's something about his face that doesn't seem right, but I can't put my finger on it. Something weird. But at least it isn't my tormentor. Why is he just standing there? Is it shock? Do I look that dishevelled? How would I have reacted to seeing something like this?

I feel hope, and joy, wake into life. *Does it matter who it is?*

'Help me,' I say. 'I've been kidnapped, I'm being held here.' Just the chance to say the words out loud feels like a lifeline. *Is it over? Am I about to get out of here?*

Something, though, is wrong: the man just stands there, staring. I don't know what to say, or what to do. *Why won't he help me?*

Then the man starts grabbing at his face and ... pulls it off.

I shudder violently. At first I can't make sense of what's going on, but then I see: it's Martin.

Martin, who has just removed a very realistic Latex mask.

Surprise. Then more bottomless disappointment. Despair. *How can anyone do this to a fellow human being?*

Martin sniggers. 'You should've seen your face.' He starts laughing. 'You looked so surprised!' He waves the mask around. 'Isn't it realistic?' Now he looks proud of himself, as though he's done something impressive.

When I don't manage a reply he just shrugs and traipses out again, the Latex mask flapping limply in his hand.

*

I'm lying awake, curled up in bed, staring at the red digits on the clock radio alarm. I'm getting great big bags under my eyes yet I still can't sleep. It's now half-one in the morning. I'm going to get out for a while in a few hours' time before Martin goes to work. My world has shrunk so much that I realise I'm experiencing genuine gratitude for that. Tears start rolling, slowly and silently, down my face. My nose, my cheeks, my temples and the pillow all get wet. I miss everything so much it makes my stomach hurt. Everyone. My freedom. Mum ...

If I do get the chance to escape when I go for a shower, I have to take it.

So eventually, as I lie there visualising what it might take to slip from my kidnapper's clutches, I fall into a fitful, anxious sleep on the sodden pillow.

I dream incredibly vivid dreams about being kidnapped, that I'm being held and I can't escape. I spot a high window and the guy holding me leaves. I see my chance to flee and the feeling when I realise I'm going to make it is just sensational. *And I do!* I open the window, clamber through and I'm outside! *What a feeling!*

Then I wake up. I stare up at the ceiling and realise that I haven't made it after all – I'm still stuck here, in the bunker.

***

The sun, the people, the weather ... I'd missed all of it, like you would not believe! This time I'd travelled alone, and to expand my horizons I was heading for Sydney, not Melbourne. The feeling I had, though, was the same. As soon as the sun's rays hit my pale skin I knew: I really did belong in the heat. My experience of the industry was that getting a job, even at one of the better clubs, was pretty straightforward, and before too long I was back in a wonderful rhythm of sunshine, swimming and hectic nights at work. I was twenty-three and living the dream. Every now and then I would stop and think to myself how lucky I was. The freedom that I had dreamed of back in Uddevalla – both in terms of having time to myself and being financially independent – was mine now, and it was all down to my own efforts. I felt strong, ready to take on whatever life was about to throw at me. When I wasn't working, I was making the most of everything Australia had to offer.

One day, after a few lovely hours on the beach, I sat down at a café as I was on my way back to the hotel for a shower. Thanks to my line of work, nights spent in shabby hostels were a thing of the past, now I was living it up in nice places with great service and good food. Sitting there in the café trying to decide whether or not to make tonight a work night (imagine that!), I spotted a girl sitting a few tables away. I was almost floored by how beautiful she was. She had long, flowing, shiny hair and beautifully plump lips; her golden-brown skin glittered beneath perfect make-up. I must admit that she did look a little bit tarty, but in an appealing way. Like an adventure wrapped up in the female form, and she behaved as though she owned the place.

She has to be a stripper, I thought to myself. My curiosity had been piqued. I'd never seen her before. If she did work at a club, it must be a really exclusive one. Maybe it was time for me to move on to a new workplace? I just walked straight over, because that's the kind of girl I am.

'Hi, I couldn't help noticing you,' I said, with a smile. Starting up conversations with complete strangers is something you get very good at if you've spent some time working in a strip club.

She smiled back, a beautiful, pearly-white smile, and told me to sit down. I ordered a glass of white wine – lovely and refreshing in the heat – and after a couple of minutes we were chatting away as if we'd known each other for years. It turned out that yes, sure enough, she was a stripper – or rather she had been.

'There's a much better way to earn big money fast,' she said with a flutter of her eyelashes as her perfectly manicured fingers curled around the stem of her glass.

The adventurer in me was captivated. Maybe I sort of knew what she was about to say straight away? Whatever, I was curious.

Slogging away doing ten-hour shifts at strip clubs for peanuts was a bit too much like hard work, she said. I, meanwhile, thought that mine was about the cushiest job around – I was earning more than I had ever dreamed of and I really struggled to see what was tough about my work. Still, I wanted to know more.

'I'm an escort, honey,' she said, flashing that sparkling smile again.

I was surprised, not to mention a little confused. Of course I knew what she was saying. She called it 'escorting'. I'd heard that word before and I knew that what she was sitting there telling me, as if it was the most natural thing on earth, was that she sold sex for a living. At first I didn't know what to think, then I asked her to tell me more.

'Darling, you can work just two hours and make more money than you do in a whole night in a club. And the places they take you, the people you get to meet ... it's such an adventure. The best-paid adventure in the world.' She laughed.

I was gobsmacked. It wasn't like I was earning a pittance in the strip clubs – far from it. But were there really people prepared to pay that much for two hours' company?

'It's not all sex though,' she went on and explained how she worked through an agency. She pulled out her phone and showed me their homepage. Besides being attractive, and being in good shape, they also had strict personality criteria you had to meet. You had to be positive, easy to talk to and clever, so that you could hold your ground in conversation on any number of subjects. All because, most of the time, the job wasn't just about sex. It was often simply about being there, with those men, in various situations. It could be anything from dinner for two in a luxury eatery, big work dos to long-distance travel and red-carpet events. It was important that you were able to blend in effortlessly with those from the upper echelons of society. Then, of course, sex with the client was usually (but not always) included after the show, or the meal, the event or whatever it was you'd attended.

I was interested, no question about that, but at the same time I was torn: if stripping is taboo for many then where do we even start with this kind of thing?

I leaned back in my chair, sipping the crisp wine and listening intently as the woman explained what a typical day was like for her. There were none of the sorts of stories

I'd been expecting. I was prepared for misery and squalor – heavy-handed customers and dirty bodies. That wasn't what I heard though: instead she told me about luxury and grandeur, about respectful, extremely wealthy clients who treated her well and paid for her time as if she were made of solid gold. And the way she described it made it seem so ... simple, so easy. I started thinking that perhaps it wasn't so awful after all.

'But what if something happens?' I asked.

I pictured how you would be completely at the mercy of a stranger, maybe at his place. Anything could happen, and no one would know where you were. She managed to reassure me that it wasn't dangerous after all, that the clients were always kind and sweet. She'd been doing it for quite a while and she'd never had even a slightly uncomfortable experience. I had seen ads in various magazines too and, as with stripping, it felt like attitudes to this down in Australia were worlds away from those back in Sweden. I wasn't exactly scared of trying new things but I couldn't really imagine meeting a man, being alone with him and then just like that you're having sex – just out of nowhere. At the same time I had to admit that I'd done just that many times before, the difference being that no money changed hands. I'd chatted and drank with men in nightclubs, then gone back to their place and had sexy one-night stands – if everything clicked and I was attracted to them. So the part about my not being able to have sex with someone on the first meeting was soon revised. My head was spinning.

'It's not really sex,' the woman said, tilting her head to one side as she took a sip of wine.

At the time, I had no idea what she meant. Now I do. Because that's exactly how escorting has always felt. I know it gets called 'sex-work', but for me it has never really been about sex, except on a handful of exceptional occasions. It's difficult to explain, but it was usually more like performing. In a way, it felt almost like an extension of the strip shows.

I have had young clients and old clients, single and married men, but the average age of the customer tends to be between forty and fifty, at least in Sweden. There, the typical client is a man who has been married with kids for a long time, someone whose sex life has become monotonous and who's looking for something different and new, some excitement in what is otherwise a really mundane daily grind. Lots of customers talk about spicing things up. Of course I've thought to myself that they're bastards, some of them – going round deceiving their wives or girlfriends like that. I have sometimes felt sorry for the women, but to be perfectly honest all that is the client's responsibility, not mine.

On a handful of occasions I've met someone who is really attractive, sexy and good company – in other words someone I might definitely have been interested in if we'd met out somewhere – and on those occasions I've allowed myself to get carried away and enjoyed myself too. Every other time, I've approached it like an acting performance, one that I had down to a fine art after a while.

Perhaps many people think that those who see escorts are all ugly or elderly men who can't find a partner, but that too is way off the mark. They are ordinary guys, some of them are really good-looking, great company and can no doubt get whoever they desire, yet they still meet escorts.

Then the woman in the café said the one thing that finally persuaded me to jump in and give it a try: 'I have a lot of regular customers. You are welcome to join me, come and meet one of them.' She was inviting me to come along and meet one of her regulars, so that I could get a feel of whether this might be something for me.

I pondered it for a while, weighed up the pros and cons. My curiosity had been piqued and of course I wondered what it must be like. How it would feel. It seemed exciting and maybe trying it once, along with another girl, might actually be a pretty amazing experience?

We carried on chatting for a bit and eventually I decided that, yes, I did want to give it a try. If I didn't like it, or if I changed my mind, she promised that I could back out at any time and I'd never have to do it again.

There really was something about this woman. She seemed so worldly. So experienced, so independent ... and rich. I was thinking about the money too, of course I was. Working two hours instead of ten for the same money? Of course that was tempting. It wouldn't just give me more free time, it would also give me the chance to save up some serious capital – towards an apartment or even a house; an education perhaps. I had given some thought to studying in the US but my grades were nowhere near good enough to get me a scholarship – I was going to have to pay my way. I'd even got as far as choosing a college in Los Angeles where I was planning to study entrepreneurship. To have a large sum of money sitting in the bank would bring incredible freedom. I imagined myself heading to America, paying my rent, paying my tuition fees myself and living it up while studying and working out exactly what kind of business I was going to start. In fact, I'd already put some of the money I'd earned from stripping into investment funds. This was a much quicker way to financial independence. Yet of course I was thinking about the people around me. How they'd react if it all came out. I'd told them about working as a stripper, but this was a whole different ball game. I knew what people were going to say. That word – the awful, ugly one – was that really me?

Whore.

I think I probably realised even back then that I was going to have to keep it to myself, because, however liberated and open-minded people are, most of them still cannot see beyond that. You cease to be a person and you just become a stereotype, and one that is morally inferior to boot. From then on you can't be intelligent, great with kids or interested in art; you can't be funny or have dreams for the future. As far as they are concerned, if you've ever sold sex, all that other stuff goes out the window.

Maybe, I thought to myself, *I had an advantage in that I was doing this on the far side of the planet*. When I got home

I'd be able to say that I'd been working as a stripper the whole time. That wasn't quite as stigmatised. By then I would also have enough capital to do whatever I wanted, ready for the next stage of my life.

Chapter Six

WEDNESDAY

INTERROGATING OFFICER: *So then we come to Wednesday, and you were able to have a shower.*

ISABEL: *And he'd bought a pair of knickers, and he lent me a pair of black trousers, a t-shirt and a top.*

INTERROGATING OFFICER: *Right, so these weren't your clothes, they were ...*

ISABEL: *No, they were his.*

INTERROGATING OFFICER: *You told us earlier that when you did shower that it was in his (inaudible 35:46).*

ISABEL: *Yes, he had me in handcuffs and everything ... then we went into his house. His bathroom. And he stayed in there the whole time I was in the shower.*

EXCERPT FROM POLICE INTERVIEW WITH
ISABEL ERIKSSON

When those red digits tell me that it's 6am I give up trying to get any more sleep. I sit up in bed and wrap the covers tighter around my legs. It's cold in here. Always. So I sleep with all my clothes on. I can't just sit here staring at the plasterboard, it'll drive me mad. I can't stop thinking about what Martin said – that he's going to let me into his house today, let me have a shower.

This might be the day I escape.

I go to the toilet and then wash my face as best I can in the little hand basin. I open the fridge and grab an apple. As I take the first bite it strikes me – the nails in my pocket might fall out when I'm in the shower. I glance over at the clock again: quarter past six. He usually comes down at about half seven to take Nellie out. Today, though, I get to go with them. I put the apple down and pull the nails out. If I can get them into the shower with me … I recall practising on my own neck. If I can manage to get them out of my pocket when we're outside the bunker, and if I manage to seriously injure him then … This could be my only chance. But then again … What if the opportunity doesn't arise? What if he takes my clothes from me while I'm in the shower – to wash them or whatever – and the nails fall out? What might the punishment be if he finds them?

My mind is made up and I'm suddenly aware that I don't have much time. With my heart in my mouth, I hurry into the dark room next to mine and crouch down beside the plank. I try to push the nails back into their holes. Not so loose that they'd fall out – maybe Martin would notice – but not so well in that I'd struggle to wiggle them out again. It's a horrible feeling, as though I'm losing the one microscopic chance I might've had: my only defence. But I don't really have a choice.

Once that's done I take a look around. Nellie's awake now and she's been at the water bowl. The poor thing – it's plain to see that being in here is affecting her badly. My happy, playful crazy little girl has morphed into a quivering, whining, filthy dog, who spends most of her time asleep. I sit down on the floor with my back resting against the bed and call her over.

'Come here, poppet!' I bounce the worn-out tennis ball that Martin brought yesterday. She looks interested – even starts wagging her tail. 'I'm going to get us out of here,' I promise her for the hundredth time. Then I roll the ball along the floor so that she can go and fetch it. After a while I notice that I'm crying.

*

It's exactly seven thirty when Martin comes into the bunker. I've started reading one of the books just to pass the time but I really can't concentrate; I keep reading the same lines over and over again. The words seem to almost be jumping around on the page in front of me and I can't follow the storyline. I place *Friend of the Devil* face down on the table and turn around on the chair as Martin enters. As always when I've been doing something he wouldn't like my heart is pounding against the inside of my ribcage.

What if he's got a CCTV camera hooked up in here and knows exactly what I've been doing? That could be yet another part of his sick game. I do, however, know that I have examined every millimetre of the whole place, so that feels very unlikely. It still sends a shiver through me and I can't really shake the thought from my mind once it has occurred to me. *Is he spying on me when I'm alone in here?*

I study his expression for any sign that that might be the case – any indication that he's seen me fiddling with the nails. He looks his normal self, though: calm and composed, a cold, fixed stare. He chucks something onto the table: 'I only bought one pair because I'm going to collect your stuff soon.'

A pair of big, ugly, white cotton knickers that look like they've been bought in a supermarket. Yet I can't wait to put them on; I can't wait to feel clean.

'Right, come on then,' he says and persuades Nellie to join him. He puts her on the lead. Then it's my turn – cuffs on, every bit as humiliating as last time. He leads me out and I notice that there's a vacuum cleaner outside the door. He sees me looking at it.

'I thought you might like to do some cleaning.'

I say nothing; I am completely focused on the fact that I'm about to get outside. To feel the wind again; to see the trees and the sky. When Martin opens the door out into the little yard, it feels like I'm being lifted a few centimetres off the ground. It's early in the morning, but the sun is coming up and I see it for the first time in four whole days. Morning sunshine. The sky – what little of it I can see over the top of

128

the fence – is rippling light blue and pink. The trunks of the trees sway gently in the breeze, although the tiny yard itself is completely sheltered from the wind. Nellie barks and darts straight over to the far corner, where she crouches down to do what she has to do. I just stand there with my face turned upwards to the sky and the trees. My toes burrow into the dewy grass and even though I feel a chill it is a wonderful feeling.

'Right …' I hate his voice so much, the very sound of it makes me smaller. 'Time to go back in.'

*

During the day I pace up and down, up and down. Do a few press-ups. Some planking. Jog on the spot and a few squats to make sure that my body is strong enough, that I'm fit enough, when the time comes. Ready to fight or to flee if that's what it takes. It becomes a sort of obsession, both the working out and my diet. I mustn't eat too early and get so hungry by the time he gets back that I don't have the energy to defend myself, but then I also need to make sure I don't eat so late that I end up feeling stuffed or giving myself a stitch. My workouts need to be just right too – enough to keep my strength up but without leaving me stiff and achy so that I can't overpower him or run away.

As soon as Martin leaves me alone I eat a substantial breakfast and then I have time for lots of coffee in the slow hours that follow. I sit at the table, staring at the knickers, while the restlessness is making my skin crawl. Have I made the right decision about the nails? I don't know. I can't risk him finding them and getting so angry that he really hurts me. The punishment might be not being allowed to shower, or it could be something much, much worse.

The clock radio turns out to be a blessing and a curse, because now I find I can't help but stare at it as the minutes drag past. And all of a sudden, I can't stop thinking about my sister. She's pregnant; I wonder how she's getting on. If she knows I've gone missing she will be worried. I keep having to bat those thoughts away, they're just too heartbreaking.

Eventually he arrives. By this point I know exactly what each door sounds like: they slam loudly, because of the weight, and that noise gets clearer each time. I've even learned off by heart how many steps he takes between each of them. My heart skips a beat. These could be the last few moments I spend in captivity. *What if I do manage to knock him down once we get outside and then get away?* Even with these cuffs on I think I should be able to give him a pretty good whack. I might be able to scream and flag down a passing car, or perhaps even make it to the nearest house. I feel myself getting more and more excited, and when Martin comes in I force myself to take a few deep breaths with my back still to him – I need to make sure he doesn't notice anything different about me and I mustn't do anything suspicious. Martin throws a coat onto the table. I put it on straight away. Even if the bunker is incredibly well soundproofed, it gets freezing in here and some more clothes are very welcome.

Besides, I could end up needing it – if I don't find help straight away, I might have to sleep rough. I turn around and hold my arms out towards him.

Martin raises one eyebrow while he puts the first cuff around my right wrist. I offer him my left.

Maybe this is what he was planning to do all along; perhaps he's seen something in my eyes, I don't know. Martin doesn't put the cuff on my other hand, instead he clicks it round his own wrist, locking us together. All the excitement I have felt, and all the images, scenarios I have gone through in my mind wither and die, leaving just that same old painful despair. My shoulders sink.

Martin stretches his neck with a large circular movement – 'You can try something if you like, but you'll end up having to drag my corpse around.'

I'm too scared to respond. Was it really that obvious? Could he tell I was planning something? I mustn't forget this. I need to learn not to give anything away; I need to teach myself to shut down all my emotional responses.

'Bring the knickers,' he says and points to the white packet on the table.

Nellie can tell that we're on our way out – she runs over to the door and starts whimpering as I stuff the knickers into one of the coat's pockets.

'Can she come too?' My voice is shaky again.

'Of course not.'

I stare down at the floor. Then I feel it: contact. With our hands cuffed together, Martin slips his hand inside mine. He holds it the way you would when heading out for a stroll with the one you love. It's like clutching an awful, massive spider. My first instinct is to scream and shake myself loose, but I realise that wouldn't be much help. Instead, I stifle the tears and let him hold my hand as we slowly make our way out of the bunker.

I mustn't be an open book. I need to learn to control my expressions even though I am now very tense at the thought of finding out what it looks like outside the bunker. I need to get a good look at any potential escape routes, but without his noticing that that's what I'm doing. I can hear Nellie barking from behind the first door to close behind us.

Stay strong, poppet. I AM going to get us out of here.

Once we get outside I look around as much as possible without moving my head too much. There's no wind and it's quiet. The ground is covered in pine needles and dry leaves. A twig cracking underneath my foot makes a nearby bird take flight – I wish I could join it. Martin's hand is burning against mine. If anyone were to see us from a distance, we probably look like a couple out for a walk, hand in hand. It's only here, right up close, that you can see the cuffs.

About twenty metres further down, I see a ramshackle old farmhouse: an ancient, crumbling pile. I spot another smaller building. And as I glance briefly over my shoulder, I can see that the building I'm being held in is painted in the traditional red of Swedish country cottages. The structure, or at least its shell, is made of wood. It looks like a garage or a workshop and seems to be a lot newer and in much better nick than the house itself. I turn to face forwards again and feel the hope drain away. There are no houses visible in any direction, just forest, forest and more forest. *Where am I?* I desperately try to garner some information that I might be able to use.

'Nice forest,' I say.

He just grunts.

It's cold, about the same as Stockholm, and it feels like we're still in Sweden. The trees and everything else look sort of familiar.

'Whereabouts are we?' I try to ask in a light tone of voice, as though it was just small talk, but he's wise to it and simply shakes his head.

Does he really live here?

The paint on the façade is peeling and the timbers look like they're rotting away in places. The whole place is crooked, like it's been abandoned for years. Maybe he doesn't live here after all. Maybe he's bought this old place just for this, just to kidnap someone. I allow myself a deep breath. Martin tightens his grip on my hand.

You'll end up having to drag my corpse around.

Tears cloud my vision and I blink them away. I don't want to use my hand; I don't want him to see that I'm crying. I don't want to give him any kind of twisted satisfaction.

As we climb the steps up to the front door I look around at my surroundings once more. Nothing. Not a single house. No traffic noise. Just trees, a few outbuildings and more trees. His car is parked over by the house. I try to read the number plates but I realise that it doesn't have any. He must have seen me looking because he says: 'Obviously I've taken the plates off, what do you take me for? I've got false plates, both Dutch and Norwegian ones.'

I think that perhaps I could steal the keys.

As we enter the house the stench of an old, damp ravaged house hits me in the face and I shudder. A narrow, grey hallway ... It's just as cold in here as it is in the bunker. I start shaking as Martin leads me through a door immediately to my left and then into a bathroom, which, while it does look newer than the rest of the house, is every bit as cold.

Martin turns me around. 'I do hope you're not going to try anything now,' he says as he removes the handcuffs. 'Try to run away, that sort of thing.'

I shake my head and try to stop the tears from flowing.

In front of me is a frosted-glass shower cubicle. To the right of that is, much to my disappointment, a single tiny window. Martin immediately understands why I'm looking at it, because he points out that it's reinforced.

Even if I did manage to smash it, it would be too small – I would never get through that. I rub my right wrist with my left hand to get rid of the sensation of the cold steel that sat tightly around it until a second ago and my thoughts start racing again. *Is there a phone in the house?* I'm no longer attached to Martin, maybe if I can hit him over the head with something hard. There's nothing here though, apart from a tube of toothpaste, a toothbrush, two scratchy, threadbare towels and a toilet roll. There's not likely to be anything in the cabinet either. Next to the shower cubicle though is a wardrobe, with the door closed. *Maybe in there?*

Once again Martin's sense of what I'm thinking is spookily accurate – he leans against the wall and says: 'I'm not planning to leave you alone in here.'

I don't reply, but I do notice that my teeth have started chattering.

'Why is it so cold?'

He chuckles. 'I haven't put the heating on.'

'Why not?'

'I'm too tight.'

Great.

'The tank isn't very big either, so you'd better make it a quick shower if you don't want the hot water to run out. I'm going to have a shave in the meantime. No need to be shy – it's not as if I've never seen you naked.' He winks, turns around to face the sink and gets his shaving kit out of the bathroom cabinet.

I hesitate as I'm about to take my clothes off – I feel so completely humiliated. He puts a can of shaving foam down on the side and looks at himself in the mirror, then starts picking at his teeth. I really cannot understand how he's able to meet his own reflection every morning. I stand up straight as it dawns on me this isn't going to be the only time I have a shower, if I end up staying here any length of time. If I can pull myself together I can still collect some information here. And the less he sees me as a threat, the easier it's going to be for me to keep him in the

135

dark. Slowly, I take my clothes off. And when I step out of the filthy, stinking jeans and top, I'm shaking with cold. Shivering, hugging myself, hunched over as I stand there naked under the psychopath's hungry, probing gaze. He didn't take his eyes off me for a second while I was getting undressed. Thank God I got rid of the nails – otherwise he would surely have noticed them.

Slowly, I step into the shower cubicle. I'm covered in goosebumps and desperate for the feeling of warm water running over my whole body, which stinks of sweat and secretions and dirt. Suddenly I freeze: there's a green bottle in the shower, exactly like one I have at home. This sudden reminder of a world outside the insane existence I've been forced into here is almost more than I can take.

He peers in my direction in the mirror: 'I hope you don't mind an audience.'

'No, it's okay,' I reply, displaying as little emotion as I can while I turn the shower on.

The pleasant sensation I've been fantasising about never arrives. Sure, washing away layers of grime and scrubbing myself clean is fantastic, but I can't really enjoy it when I know that Martin is standing there staring at me the whole time. I wash my hair, wash myself thoroughly between the legs; I wash my whole body. And I do it quickly. I can feel Martin's stare through the frosted glass. When I'm done, I hurry out and put the knickers on straight away. They're too big, but it's still a great feeling. Martin watches me dry myself, then opens the wardrobe.

'You can borrow some of my clothes. I'll put yours in the wash.'

He holds out a pair of black tracksuit bottoms, a t-shirt and a jumper.

I put them all on as fast as I can. They're too big so it's pretty obvious that they're his clothes.

'Look at this.' He points to a pair of shoes that are lying in the wardrobe and strokes a coat that's hanging in there. He looks proud of himself. 'This is top-quality gear, not exactly the sort of thing you get from an army surplus shop. And that sleeping bag –' he points to the bottom shelf '– is rated for really low temperatures. Which is good, because you never know.'

I really don't know why, but it's pretty obvious that he wants me to note all of this and to react, so I say something along the lines of: 'Wow, impressive.'

Once I've dried my hair on one of the scratchy towels, Martin handcuffs us together again. My heart sinks: this was my chance, the one that I have been longing for all day, and now it's gone.

'Are you hungry?' he asks as we're making our way across the yard back towards the bunker. Just the sight of the little red building puts my stomach in knots and sends despair hopping through my chest. I don't actually feel hungry in the slightest, but I realise that eating would be the smart thing to do, so I say yes. I also try to gulp down as many lungfuls of the fresh outdoor air as I can. Who knows when I'll next be able to breathe clean air?

'I'm going to go and have a shower myself. Tell you what, you do some readymade corned beef hash and fried eggs – we can eat together?' he says, once the last of the doors has slammed behind us and we're back inside my prison.

I tell him that that'll be fine.

He nods at the packet of birth control pills that he's brought out with him along with the vitamins and the supplements I asked for. 'You'll have to start taking those every day. Same sort you're on now.'

'Do we have to ... have unprotected sex? Can't we use condoms?'

He sniggers and tells me that he most definitely does not want to use condoms and a thought that strikes me now is like staring into the abyss.

'What if ... imagine if I get pregnant anyway?'

Martin licks his front teeth with the tip of his tongue. 'I'm a doctor,' he beams. 'I can take care of the delivery.' He gives me a look that sends shivers through my entire body, right down to the tips of my toes. A disgusting look, as though he would actually like us to have children together.

I swallow hard. Don't say a word as I let Martin take the handcuffs off me and Nellie jumps up against my legs to greet me. I remember reading about Josef Fritzl and how he held his daughter captive for years. How she'd got pregnant after he raped her, and how the child – or maybe there was more than one? – had grown up as a prisoner. Is that the fate that's waiting for me? All those dreams about meeting Mr Right, about settling down somewhere with my own stable or moving to America to study or start a family are now torturing my soul. I don't want to give birth in here, all alone in a dusty, soundproofed bunker. I don't want to be locked up in here, day after day, watching my child grow up with no idea of what the world outside looks like.

'If you do some food I'll be back after my shower.'

I can barely hear the words. All I can think of is him saying we're going to sleep together tonight and his words are playing on a loop inside my head.

I can take care of the delivery.

*

The plates are on the table. The corned beef hash. The beetroot. The eggs I've fried on the little cooking ring. I've managed to do all of it without burning anything. I've taken my pill and I've prayed to God. Now Martin and I are sitting next to each other on the same side of the table and I feel anaesthetised. He's asked a few questions and I've given the most neutral answers I could manage. Mechanically I've picked up food with my fork, lifted it to my mouth, chewed, swallowed and then repeated the whole process time and time again. He doesn't seem the least bit bothered by the whole situation, quite the opposite. I've made him some food. Now he can talk away and just take it easy. Then we're going to go to bed together. It is exactly the kind of fucked-up relationship he's been hoping for all along. How can anyone get so far removed from reality? Just how sick is this guy?

You're one to talk, aren't you? Sitting here, eating dinner and making small talk with the psychopath who's kidnapped you.

I remind myself of my strategy. Keep it neutral. Compliant. At the same time I'm struggling to keep the food down when I think to myself that he might want to have sex with me today. And tomorrow. At least two or three times a day. I have never had sex with anyone against my will. Never. Not once. Not at work, nor in my private life. In relationships, if ever I've felt like not having sex, I've said so. And I've chosen which customers to sleep with, and when. And now I am sitting here, trying to mentally prepare myself for being raped. Perhaps on a daily basis, several times a day. I put my fork down. I can't manage another bite and I'm battling the nausea.

Martin rubs his tummy. 'That was nice.' Then he reaches into his pocket and pulls out two slightly squashed truffles in little red wrappers. He opens one and pops it in his mouth, then gives me the other one. Instantly, alarm bells start ringing: the strawberries. I look at the little chocolate in my hand. Hesitate. What do I do now? Imagine if he's trying to drug me again? He's already told me that he raped me last time. Is that what turns him on? Being in bed with an unconscious woman? He obviously likes the idea of my being here, completely defenceless and at his mercy. This is his idea of a perfect relationship.

'You don't have to eat it,' Martin says. 'I know what you're thinking.'

I put the truffle on the table and lay my hands in my lap. But when he looks put out, I pick it up again and eat it – I don't want to make him angry. I'm anxious, terrified of what might happen next. Incredibly tense but doing my best to hide it.

'Right, it's getting late. Time for some sleep.' Martin stands up and takes our plates over to the sink. He then gets undressed while I stay sitting and watch. Right down to his boxers. I can see the outline of his manhood against the fabric and he's clearly aroused.

He said sleep though, nothing else. That gives me an ounce of hope. It really is late and tomorrow he's going to drive up to Stockholm to collect my stuff. Maybe he genuinely just wants to sleep tonight. Even so, the idea of getting into bed with this man, the one who has taken everything away from me and locked me inside this filthy, windowless bunker, is enough to make my skin crawl.

He must've noticed my hesitation because he tells me to keep my knickers on if it makes me feel better. Then he gets into bed, under my duvet, and holds it up for me. Then suddenly it looks as though something's just occurred to him. He puts his hand under the pillows and pats around, as though he is looking for something. 'You haven't hidden anything here, have you? A fork or something like that? I just hope you don't get any silly ideas ...'

I just shake my head.

'You lie on the inside – I'm getting up early. That way I won't disturb you when I'm getting up.'

As if I'm going to get any sleep, I want to hiss, but I manage to chomp my mouth shut before the words come out. The looks he gives me as I'm getting undressed make me feel sick again. As he studies all of my movements, his eyes light up. I know exactly what's going on. I've seen that look so many times before: he's getting turned on.

My legs are trembling as I clamber over my kidnapper and get into bed, as close to the wall as I possibly can and avoiding any body contact. The tears are threatening to come at any moment and, once again, I'm absolutely terrified. If he wants to have sex but I don't go along with it, what'll he do then? Murder me? Make the torture jokes into reality? I'm not going to have a choice; I'm going to have to. I feel a hand stroking my upper arm, then, out of nowhere Martin violently thrusts his arm in under my body so that he's holding me, then pulls me tightly against him. He smells clean, because he's just had a shower, but I hate the smell of him anyway.

'Lie down with your head on my chest,' he orders.

I daren't disobey. He carries on stroking my arm and my shoulder while my heart is pumping so hard it makes me dizzy. Every touch feels like great big insects crawling around on my skin. He takes my hand and puts it to his neck. Then he moves it around his body, shoving it from his cheek and neck and down over his chest, as if I was stroking him. I just don't want him to push it any further down, and to try to make him think about something else I say: 'Wouldn't it be better if … if you had a proper girlfriend instead? One that you love and who loves you?'

He stiffens up and lets go of my hand. 'Why?'

Dare I? I must. However much I've promised myself to stay neutral, I can't muster the force to keep myself from saying what I feel.

'How good do you think it is, compared to having someone ... imprisoned? It will never be the same.'

For a long time he stays silent and I can tell I've touched a nerve. But I manage to pluck up the courage.

'It can never be the same as having a real girlfriend, this, me. You do know that, don't you?' I strain to keep my voice gentle and my tone friendly.

'We can talk about it another time,' he replies after another long pause. Then he grabs my hand again and puts it on his chest.

'Did you ... hmm,' he starts, hesitantly, '... have any ... plans? For the future? I mean before ... all this?'

At first I'm lost for words. Why does he want to know that? Is this just yet another way of tormenting me? By making me think about everything I've ever dreamed of but will now, if he has his way, never be able to do? I tell him about wanting to study in America if I can get into a good college. That otherwise I plan on setting up on my own – a day kennel maybe, one where I offer a collection and dropping-off service, because, as far as I know, none of the others does that.

'That's very ... ambitious. You seem to have given it a lot of thought,' he says, apparently surprised at the idea that someone like me might have plans at all.

'Yes, of course I have,' I reply. 'I've been planning to stop escorting. I've been thinking about it for a while. After all, I'm thirty now and it's time to realise my dreams. That's ... that's what I was thinking.'

Should I carry on? It's impossible not to.

'If you do keep me here for a few years though, I don't know what's going to happen to me. I have the same dream as you do. Find someone to marry. Someone I love. Have kids. What if I'm too old by the time you ... let me go?'

He gulps. 'You can have children later in life now. Having a child at forty is no problem.'

Is he trying to tell me he's changed his mind? No longer a couple of years now, but ten? For ages, I can't get a single word out. After a while, Martin says: 'What did you do for your eighteenth birthday?'

'I ... I ... well ... Like most people, I guess. I had a party and then we went out.'

He makes a noise that is somewhere between mocking laughter and a sneeze. 'Like most people. Yes. Exactly. Hmm ... We've talked about ... my little defect. Yes, down there, haven't we?'

I nod, my head still lying on his chest. I feel his heart beating against my cheek. I can hardly believe it – if I'd had to guess, I would've said that he didn't have a heart at all. But now I notice that his heart is beating harder too. I've touched a nerve again.

'On my eighteenth birthday,' Martin says, now sounding almost upset, 'I had a series of operations. Down there ... As a child, I suffered from a very unusual condition – we can do the anatomy lecture another time – but, as you've seen, the operations didn't really go as planned. Because of that, I've never been able to have a "proper girlfriend", as you put it. No one wants to be with me.'

Anatomical defect? Last time he told me that it was an old military injury. I don't know what to believe. Is he lying? Toying with me? Or is this actually the truth?

'Guess when I last had sex?' he says.

'Saturday. With me, when I was unconscious,' I say, and I can't disguise the sharpness in my voice.

'No, before that. With a normal girl who was interested in me, I mean. Not an escort.'

'I don't know, a couple of weeks before that?'

A bitter laugh. 'You might've thought so. No, it was seven years ago.'

'Woah,' is the only reply I can think of.

He straightens up a bit in bed and sort of burrows his back into the mattress. I am just grateful that he doesn't seem turned on anymore.

'There were a few girls, five or six, back when I was younger. I tried to keep the sex thing out of it for as long as I could. But when we finally did have sex, they dumped me. All of them.'

Is he really expecting me to lie here and feel sorry for him?

If he understands how much pain being dumped can cause someone, how on earth can he not understand the trauma of someone being abducted and locked up against their will by a complete stranger?

145

'But ...' I begin, but he cuts me off.

'No one is ever going to want me. That's all I want: a relationship.'

I stare up at the corrugated steel ceiling. Might I be able to talk my way out of this? It's worth a try. I take a deep breath of dusty air, then give him the best lying I can manage:

'I don't think you should give up. You're a catch. Good-looking. You're a doctor. That thing ... down there, it's just a detail. When you meet the right girl, she won't give it a second glance. A girl who loves you.'

Martin looks at me. 'Do you think?'

'Yes.' The hope stirs in my chest yet again. If I can persuade him that, yes, he can find himself a proper girlfriend, then maybe he'll let me go. 'You mustn't give up. You've been unlucky with a handful of girls, but there are millions of women out there, even just in Sweden. I'm certain you'll be able to find the right one. Not like this, with me, but ... normal. One who falls in love with you and wants to get married, have kids. You've got everything going for you.'

Apart from the fact that you're a psycho who drugs and kidnaps women, I think to myself, but then I carry on: 'I was actually looking forward to meeting you, on that Saturday. And we'd already had sex by then, hadn't we? I didn't even think about that, down there. I just thought you were a nice guy that I was happy to meet again.'

Careful now, my inner voice warns. *Don't overdo it. If he falls in love with you and you've said all these things then he's definitely not going to want to let you go.*

I go quiet; I need to choose my words carefully.

After a while Martin sighs heavily. 'Well, that's your opinion. And you seem to be the only one who thinks like that. All the others have dumped me once they've seen it.'

I suspect that I might not be getting the whole truth, but from his point of view that's what happened. If he hasn't had sex with them straight away, they're going to have had time to start getting to know him. Maybe these girls just sensed that there's something not quite right about this psychopath and then just used his deformity as an excuse. After all, who wants to dump someone with the words: 'No, you make me feel uneasy. You seem like a real head case'? They've probably just withdrawn and then used the penis thing to get out of it altogether. Obviously I can hardly tell him that.

'I don't think you should give up,' I say instead.

'Almost always immediately after sex . . .' Martin says. His voice is cracking. 'Why do you think I've found myself sitting there, with that pistol in my mouth, fifty times?'

His breathing is getting faster and faster, then suddenly he clenches his fist and punches himself in the chest. I go stiff with fear, then I see that he's crying. Despite all the tears he's caused me – and how all my distress has left him completely unmoved – for a second I feel sorry for him. He goes tense, then punches again. This time he makes contact both with himself and with me. My heart is pounding. I need to get him to calm down. I've never seen him this angry, this frustrated, and I don't want to see him any worse. Don't want to see what he might be capable of. I am so desperate that I move towards him. I put my arms around him, but say nothing. For a long time he stays quiet too, but slowly his breathing gets calmer. He lies staring at the ceiling as I stare at the red digits on the display: it's 1am.

'Shouldn't we get some sleep?' I attempt, despite knowing that I almost certainly won't get a minute's sleep as long as I'm sharing a bed with him.

If I do make it out of here, will I ever be able to sleep with anyone again?

That's a question I cannot answer. Grief swells up inside me. Imagine if he does keep me here until I die. *What if this is the last man I'm ever going to sleep with, while the rest of the world thinks I'm dead, or that I've disappeared of my own free will?*

Martin checks the time himself. 'Yes, that's probably a good idea,' he says. He rolls onto his side and pulls me towards him so that we're spooning each other. I feel it straight away: he is hard. It's pushing against my bottom. I go completely stiff and I daren't move – I don't want to encourage him or give him any reason to think that I want to have sex. After a few minutes, all my muscles are aching because I'm straining my whole body and my breathing is fast and shallow.

After a while though, Martin seems to fall asleep. His breathing gets deeper, but I don't allow myself to believe it. Maybe he's just acting, to see how I respond? The pain in my left side just keeps getting worse. As carefully, as gently as I possibly can, I turn over so that I end up on my back instead. At first I count the seconds, then the minutes. And when I start aching again, from lying there stiff and tense, I roll over again.

Martin wakes up instantly, and puts his hand on my shoulder. As though he's trying to stop me from going anywhere.

***

Butterflies. In my stomach. No, that doesn't do it justice. Huge, mutant, monster butterflies! My whole body was buzzing as we got into the taxi that was going to take us to my glamorous new friend's regular client.

Just before we left, she'd explained a few things to bear in mind. Using protection went without saying – condoms were a must. Not only that, it was a good idea to give his penis a quick inspection once his clothes came off. Make sure it didn't look weird – no warts or anything. If the customer took me for dinner, or drinks, beforehand, I should remember to only have a glass or two of wine, because it's important to keep a clear head. She also told me to make sure I always had some lube with me, because I probably wasn't going to actually get turned on. At least she never did – no matter how well she knew the client, or liked him, it was still a job. She told me to think of it as acting. Moan, sure, but don't overdo it. Faking an orgasm close to the end was another tip. If the customer was struggling to cum, your best bet was usually to pretend to enjoy yourself, she explained. This was a job and you had to be creative sometimes.

At that moment though – sitting in the taxi on the way to my first ever appointment as an escort – I was still a bit ... maybe not sexually aroused, but ... excited. This was a big step, and it was exhilarating. It felt like the start of a new adventure: this was something forbidden, something taboo, and the excitement sent tingles over my skin. It was early evening and despite it still being warm outside my skin was covered in goosebumps.

We arrived at the house, which was surrounded by a lush garden, and it was plain to see that whoever lived here was very comfortably off. I gulped and straightened my top. Should I have gone for something other than denim shorts, maybe something a bit more glamorous? But my mentor quickly reassured me that I'd got it just right. She was wearing an informal summer dress herself.

The client was a man of about forty-five. He shook my hand and greeted me politely as he showed us through to his sun terrace. It was summer and sitting there by his pool, surrounded by trees, bushes and palms, felt a little bit like sitting in the middle of a rainforest – lush and intimate and beautiful. After chatting for a while, I could see that he was kind and respectful, and my nervousness began to evaporate. We hadn't been there very long when he produced two envelopes and gave one to both of us. I can't actually remember exactly how much he paid, but I think it was around about a thousand dollars each. We were going to spend two hours there. I stuffed the envelope into my handbag and I could hardly take it in. He poured us a glass of champagne each and we carried on chatting away on the terrace. That wasn't what I'd been expecting either. I guess I'd expected the client to be a little bit more 'straight to the point' and keen to make sure he spent as much of the time he'd paid for as possible actually having sex. Once again, I'd got it wrong. The average customer is looking for what the agencies call *GFE – The Girlfriend Experience*. They want to chat for a while, create an atmosphere. They want to have a drink together, share a laugh and talk about themselves, the day they've had or they might be curious about you, yet the atmosphere stays flirty and everyone knows exactly where the evening is going to end up. Customers don't want it to feel like they're paying for it – they want it to feel like an ordinary date. Flirting with strangers is something you get down to a fine art after working in a strip club for a while, so it wasn't really a problem for me to take on the role. I watched everything the other woman did intently – what she said, how she moved, and I mimicked her as I sipped the sparkling drink.

After a while, the mood changed, as though the air was getting warmer even though the sun was going down, and we all moved into the bedroom. The butterflies were back in a flash. It was happening; I was going to do it. I looked over at the client. There was nothing wrong with him – handsome, worldly, respectful and polite. He was well groomed and well dressed. And you could tell that he was very excited. You could also tell that my mentor knew exactly what she was doing as she took control of the situation, while my role was just to play along.

She pulled him towards her. I could see the bulge in his trousers. She stroked him, moving her body against his like a cat, and he responded to her touch. Then he sat himself down on the bed as she came over towards me. Tentatively, we started touching each other. She smelled like summer and the look in her eyes made me relax and feel secure. Before long I found myself really getting into the role and realised that I was actually enjoying it. Being a sexual goddess, moving so sensually that the man was almost beside himself with desire, saying the right things, pouting with moist lips ... this wasn't demanding or unpleasant, not by any means. I didn't get turned on, but this was definitely not an unsavoury experience.

My mentor gave an incredibly sensual performance while making clear that she had very definite boundaries. I'm glad that she was with me for my first time because it made me realise that there was absolutely nothing wrong with sticking hard to certain rules; that it didn't kill the mood or make things awkward. Right from the start, from that first time, I've also been very strict about my own boundaries and I've never had any problem maintaining them with customers. I've never had anal sex, no 'rough sex', BDSM or agreed to anything that I'm not comfortable doing. I've always made sure to use protection and I've always been careful with hygiene, to minimise the risks of catching any kind of illness.

It was all over pretty quickly. It was a threesome – he had sex with both of us, changing condom in between, obviously, and during the act I kept thinking about everything she'd told me about what noises to make, how to act, and I found myself really getting into the part.

WEDNESDAY

Even afterwards, the atmosphere was still relaxed. For my part, I was most pleased about having earned so much money so easily, and that really was how it felt: easy. Much better than ten hours' stripping. That was it – from then on I never wanted to go back to that job. Now, I decided, I was an escort.

Chapter Seven

THURSDAY

INTERROGATING OFFICER: *Any thoughts about what might happen if you happened to have an accident that meant you couldn't get back to the bunker, while she's locked in there?*

MARTIN TRENNEBORG: *How do you mean . . .?*

INTERROGATING OFFICER: *If you were to have an accident, on the way home from work, for example.*

MARTIN TRENNEBORG: *Uh huh.*

INTERROGATING OFFICER: *Isabel's locked in the bunker.*

MARTIN TRENNEBORG: *As a matter of fact that had occurred to me.*

INTERROGATING OFFICER: *And what were your thoughts?*

MARTIN TRENNEBORG: *Well, I could've prepared a note of some kind. Not something I've done as yet. But I could've left a note, well, amongst my accounts or whatever. Just something to explain the situation, simple as that. That sort of thing might've been necessary if I'd, I don't know, ploughed into an elk at one-twenty and died.*

INTERROGATING OFFICER: *Pardon?*

MARTIN TRENNEBORG: *Well, if I hit an elk at that kind of speed and die, then someone's bound to be interested in tying up all my affairs. I mean, sell the house, the car, all those sorts of things. Then I could have a letter in a sealed envelope, so it would show if someone had opened it, you know, someone snooping around or whatever. I could've prepared that, but it wasn't something I'd got round to.*

EXCERPT FROM INTERVIEW WITH
MARTIN TRENNEBORG

Morning once more. My fifth day in the clutches of this psychopath. I lie in bed, pressed against the wall, trying to avoid contact with his body, but it's basically impossible. When I lie on my side, he lies there and pushes himself against me, or else, if I lie on my back, he'll put his arm around me. He's spent the whole night with one arm under my neck. I can't avoid his touch unless I get out of bed – which I don't dare do. He set the alarm for seven and has actually had a fair bit of sleep. I, on the other hand, have been awake for most of the night. For the last hour or two I've noticed him being awake a bit more because he's been looking at the clock every now and then. I close my eyes, pretending to be asleep; I just want him to go. By now my family must have noticed that I've gone missing and they'll have called the police. I've never ever been away for this long without telling anyone where I am. I usually stay in touch with the people I care about even when I'm abroad and working. I dearly hope that something is going on, out there in the world outside while I'm lying here, terrified. I hope they're looking. Perhaps they've been to the apartment and taken fingerprints? Maybe they've found my phone? There must be a way to find me. Somehow.

Finally, the alarm goes off and Martin opens his eyes. Just as I suspected, he's already wide awake.

'Good morning,' he says.

It really isn't.

'Good morning.'

Mercifully he sits up and swings his legs out of bed straight away. He's done with the snuggling. He rubs the back of his neck a few times with a big yawn.

'Are you ...' I begin cautiously, '... off to Stockholm today?'

Nellie, who has been curled up under the table for the first time since we've been here, comes out and stretches her legs, never taking her eyes off Martin. She goes over to her water bowl and has a few slurps, then sits herself down by the door and starts whining.

'Uh huh,' is Martin's only response. He stands up, puts his shirt and trousers on and puts Nellie on the lead.

When the door slams shut behind them, I immediately leap out of bed. I pull on the tracksuit bottoms and t-shirt I was given yesterday. Not being allowed to go with them today is hard to take. I look at the clock – five past seven. That means that the sun will be coming up out there. I close my eyes and try to see the colours of dawn breaking on the backs of my eyelids.

I've taken so much in life for granted.

Just a few minutes later, Martin returns. I'm lying on the bed again and, now that it's just me, Nellie jumps straight up and snuggles down in my lap. I nuzzle into her coat and breathe – I can smell the fresh air.

'It's going to be a long day,' Martin says. I notice that he's brought the vacuum cleaner that has been on the other side of the door in with him. 'I'll have breakfast at mine, then I'll get in the car.'

'Right,' I say, picturing him arriving at the apartment only to be greeted by two burly policemen who've had the place under surveillance.

'I don't know whether I'll be back tonight or first thing tomorrow.'

'What do you mean?'

Is he going to sleep in my apartment? Has he got the balls to do that?

He sneers in that way he does when he's playing games with me. 'You never know. But as soon as I get back, I'll take you outside.'

Take me outside. I'm just like Nellie. A pet.

158

When he finally leaves I feel the tiredness overwhelming me. For days, I've been sleeping three or four hours a night, and last night I got a couple of short naps, fifteen or twenty minutes at best. Surprisingly, perhaps, I prefer being alone in here, completely cut off, to having to have anything to do with Martin.

'Come here, poppet,' I say and pat the bed next to where I'm lying under the covers.

Nellie gets into bed too and snuggles right up to me. I can feel her little breaths on my stomach and her coat tickles me a bit. And – this is the miracle of being a human being – lying there, my eyes closed, with my beloved dog finally able to relax next to me, I smile. Only for a second, but a smile nonetheless. With one arm wrapped around Nellie, I drift off while praying to God that He'll let Martin get caught today.

*

The next time I open my eyes, it's 11am. *Maybe Martin will have got there by now?* That thought fills me with hope again and my body responds with a restlessness that makes me get straight out of bed to get some breakfast for the two of us.

Please, God, let him get caught today, please, God, let them catch him and find me today.

And if they don't catch him, if Martin does come back, and I see that he's brought all of my things, I've already decided what to do then. I don't know how, or when, I suppose the next time I get to shower. Then there'll be no more neutral, compliant Isabel, no more model prisoner act. I'll use the nails. Give it all I've got. Kill or be killed. Because the idea of my being in this hellhole for 'a couple of years or so' is absolutely out of the question. That would send me completely insane. At the same time, the voice inside my head is telling me that of course it's not going to be 'a couple of years' at all. How would that work? Would he just let me go and trust me not to go to the police? No chance. It's more likely that once he gets bored of me he'll murder me after all.

I do some exercises after breakfast. I read standing up – I just can't get comfortable sitting down. Subconsciously, I'm waiting for the doors to be opened at any minute. Not by Martin, but by the police. Eventually the restlessness makes me plug in the vacuum cleaner that Martin brought. It can't be healthy for me or Nellie to be constantly breathing in all this dust, dust that coats every surface in here, and besides, keeping myself busy will pass the time. I start by the door, making sure to hoover up all the dust I can get at, but I don't get the chance to do more than about five minutes before the thing conks out on me. I straighten up. Turn it off and on again. Nothing. I try pulling the plug out and putting it back in a few times, but still nothing happens. Then I turn to look around the room.

No!

The nightlight is off, as is the clock radio. I've managed to blow a fuse. Luckily, it looks as though there are two circuits because the ceiling light is still on. If not for that, it would be pitch-black. Now I'm left with no sense of time whatsoever. I cry out and throw the vacuum cleaner to one side, then sit down on the bed and start eating a banana. It must be about twelve noon. *The next time I get hungry, it should be about five*, I think to myself. I'm going to have to trust my body clock completely and feel my way through.

After reading for what seems like a couple of hours, I have some more food – the hotplate is still working, thank God. I reheat some meatballs and a bit of pasta. Then Nellie gets a few meatballs and after that I start pacing up and down with one of the books in my hands.

When it gets to what I guess is about 10pm, I think to myself that it's probably a good thing that he hasn't come back. It might mean they've arrested him. By this point I'm feeling more and more tired, but I'm not sure whether or not I should be going to bed. It might be nine o'clock, or it could be one in the morning, I really have no idea.

Eventually I stop pacing and get into bed, switch off the light. It goes completely dark. Occasional humming from the fridge is the only sound inside the confined space and I lie there staring into space, wavering between hope and despair. I try to mentally prepare myself for Martin coming back with my stuff and me having to fight for my life. One minute I feel strong, ready to face him, kill or be killed. The next I'm so overwhelmed with fear that I can hardly breathe. Convinced that I won't manage to escape, and that I'm going to be raped, tortured and then murdered. I feel I've ended up in hell on earth, in this living nightmare.

Nellie starts rummaging around in the bed, pawing my head as if she just can't get close enough. It's obvious that she doesn't like it being so dark. I peel up a corner of my duvet and let her lie down right up against me and stroke her little back as I whisper a few comforting words. When it seems like she's calmed down, I start praying again. I pray for so long, so intently, that, when I finally fall asleep, I do so with my hands tightly clasped together.

***

The woman who had taken me on my first job gave me lots of tips about various agencies and there were ads from plenty of others in magazines. So I just got straight down to it and started ringing around. Before too long I'd started working for some of the most exclusive agencies. The customers paid unbelievable sums for an hour, an evening or a whole night, and they expected you to not only look good, but to be sophisticated enough to accompany them on all kinds of occasions.

Most of the agencies had their own apartments in central Sydney. These were lavishly furnished places where you could go and wait for the agency to send another customer – effectively on call, ready to head off if the call came. Just as with stripping, it was completely up to you whether you wanted to work or not on any given night, and it was of course perfectly fine to decline a particular customer or assignment. The majority of clients called in the evening or at night, and the agencies were keen to make sure that you were in the apartment. That way they could be sure that you were all made up, hair done and ready to work at the drop of a hat. Everything had to be of the very highest standard. Sometimes the customers would have very particular requests, like what colour stockings they wanted you to wear or they would ask for a certain kind of underwear or dress. The dresses had to be sexy, yet classy – no one was supposed to be able to tell you were an escort if you were going for a meal at a top restaurant, or dinner with the boss. Beautiful, high-heeled shoes were a must, as was a classy handbag containing lube and condoms in various sizes. We also had handheld card terminals, in case the customer preferred to pay that way. If the customer wanted a home visit, the agencies would arrange lovely chauffeur-driven limos to take you there and then pick you up again at whatever time you arranged.

All that helped to make me feel a lot more secure. They always checked customers' identities and if you were visiting someone at home the agency would always make sure that the person really did live at that address. If you were booked to go to a hotel room, they'd check with reception to make sure they'd been given a real name and that there actually was a reservation in that name. Of course none of this was free – the agencies took half the fee – but even so, the amounts I was earning were quite astonishing compared to what stripping paid, not to mention the wages I'd had back in Sweden. Of course you could always try to get the client to extend the booking – usually if they'd booked an hour you could get them to pay for another one, and sometimes the whole night.

Sometimes I'd be hanging around in the apartment waiting for a call but nothing would turn up. But that wasn't exactly a great hardship. It meant spending the evening in a luxury apartment in the centre of town, watching TV between seven in the evening and three in the morning. Doing manicures and putting my hair up, surfing my favourite websites. Other times, it'd be non-stop, toing and froing from one client to the next. Lots of these men lived in incredible homes, which made going to work even more fun. Seeing how the seriously wealthy lived was really quite an eye-opener. Most of the time, I would spend a couple of hours on a booking. A glass of wine maybe, or perhaps the client might've cooked dinner or bought nibbles. I would sit by the pool, or on a sea-view terrace, sipping wine and talking about everything under the sun until it was time to have sex. Usually it would just be once, but if the client had booked the whole night we would sometimes do it twice. It always started with my getting my fee, and then we might head off to some posh restaurant for three courses and some great wine. Sometimes, if the client felt the need to be discreet, we would have dinner at home. Afterwards we would head for the bedroom or the hotel room and have sex.

I know that some escorts will have sex several times in a night, but as far as I was concerned, once or twice was plenty. Then we'd sleep together, and actually that's the bit that sometimes felt a bit weird. You're very vulnerable while you're asleep and sometimes clients would want to snuggle up for a cuddle, which was something I really didn't like. That felt like a private part of my life that I didn't want to share. I would usually let them do it for a short while, then say that I needed my beauty sleep – and they always got the message. After a whole evening and a long night, both the client and I were usually asleep pretty quickly. Occasionally I might have a quickie in the morning before we got dressed and ate breakfast. At 9am the 'whole night' was officially over and I would head home.

Without fail, my clients behaved like perfect gentlemen. Most of the time they were older than me and very interesting to talk to. I was in a position where I could learn something new from every conversation.

Once, a regular paid for me to go to Florida on holiday with him. He paid about seventy thousand kronor for the week. He had this fantastic apartment and he told me he spent a lot of time there every winter. We flew out first class and every day that week he asked me what I would like to do. We spent the time shopping, sunbathing and swimming, eating at the best restaurants and enjoying each other's company. By that time he had been a regular of mine for two years and he was very good-looking. He had kids, but was divorced. He was always out partying, dating lots of girls, and each time we met up he would talk about the dates, always being completely frank, especially if he thought he might've met someone special. I think he thought it was nice to be able to open up to me about anything and I would let him know how I thought he should deal with his 'girl problems'. He bought me jewellery, necklaces and earrings worth hundreds and hundreds of dollars, and whenever we met he would never fail to tell me how beautiful and how wonderful I was. He often said that no one he'd ever met would match up to me, and nor would anyone he was going to meet. I guess that meant he was really quite fond of me, but he knew from the start that nothing was ever going to come of it; that I wasn't interested in him outside of our business arrangement. I'd made sure I made that perfectly clear in a friendly but unmistakable way right at the outset.

The week in Florida was great fun at first, but before too long being with him started to feel like a chore – it was a job, after all, and I had to constantly play the part of perfect company. There was no place for 'having a bad day' given how much he had paid – I had to stay happy, positive and sensual for twenty-four hours a day, for seven days on the trot.

I learned to adapt to each client's personality. If they had a calm nature, I'd be calm too; if they were big talkers then I would chat away. It wasn't that difficult to get a handle on customers, to find out what they wanted from me. I would usually start off just being myself but I would then quickly adapt to the particular customer's needs – both as a companion in public and in the bedroom.

The guy who took me to Florida once told me that he wanted to marry me. He explained that I'd be able to stay at home and that he'd give me a monthly allowance of thousands of dollars. I knew that I'd never be able to marry for money though. Any doubts I might have had had been dispelled by that week in the States. Being perfect company for an hour or two, or the odd night, was one thing, doing it around the clock was something entirely different. It just wouldn't feel right, and a life like that would never make me happy, no matter how much money was involved.

Away from work, I've always tried to live as normal a life as possible and of course I've dreamed about meeting the love of my life. What use would all that money be if it meant spending your life in a loveless prison? I think that might also be why I've never struggled to separate sex at work from my own personal sex life. I have always 'saved' the enjoyment for myself, for my private life. I've never let my job affect things too much, apart from a few times when I've felt a bit bored with sex. I've never even felt bad after sex at work, nor regretted it. Not even once.

I never talked with that regular about my own private life, or with any of my other clients for that matter. I never used my real name, or revealed where I grew up, and I definitely didn't give any details about my private sex life. Sometimes I did have to make things up, just to keep the conversation going, but this man – and all the others – knew full well that this was ultimately a business transaction; that I didn't want to talk about personal stuff. It was rare for any of them to ask any really personal questions.

Life was just rolling by at quite a pleasant tempo. Sometimes I worked as an independent escort, sometimes for the various agencies. I started to get into a pattern – spending my summers in Sweden and then working in Australia for the autumn and winter. At the age of twenty-four I was able to fulfil my lifelong dream of doing a make-up artist course. My attitude towards escorting was pretty much the same as my attitude to stripping – it was never something I planned on doing forever. I always wanted to get married, have kids and live a normal life at some point.

I attended the course in the mornings and worked in the afternoons. I would always have my work phone with me and at the end of each lesson it would always show loads of missed calls. I never did apply for a single job as a make-up artist.

I spent a few years working for the most exclusive agencies in New York and Miami. In New York, I would usually visit customers at home, which most of the time meant visiting incredibly luxurious condominiums or houses. For a while there was just me and one other girl working for the top three agencies in Miami (all of which happened to have the same owners). I was tall and slim, with long blonde hair, the other girl had dark skin and was very beautiful – she had won a beauty contest just a year or so earlier. We ended up sharing an apartment with fantastic views of Miami; it was almost like a dream come true. We worked a lot, every single day. Sometimes a customer might ring and ask to meet during the afternoon, but most of the time we had the daylight hours to ourselves and we tended to spend them on the beach. Then, as the evening approached, it all swung into life. The agency owners were a very wealthy Russian couple who would come to the apartment every evening. They would usually arrive with several bookings and this always made me feel that I couldn't really say I wanted an evening off, which was a shame. Miami nightlife was amazing, and very enticing. The customers were society's supreme elite – entrepreneurs, hockey players, film directors, musicians and all kinds of stars. Needless to say, we were bound by secrecy agreements never to reveal which of them we might have met as clients.

Those were pretty good times and I earned a lot of money. Eventually though the time came for me to move on. I didn't want to work every night. It had almost started to feel like the drudgery of work back in Sweden – the lack of freedom, not being able to make your own decisions – and freedom was the whole reason for my being in that line of work in the first place. Just before my visa ran out, I quit and checked into a luxury hotel. I made the most of it and partied hard for those last few days until it was time to fly home.

*

After moving back to Sweden on a more permanent basis I carried on working as an escort, in Stockholm. I took my own photos, wrote a carefully worded ad and then published them on various escort sites online. Always I obscured my face in adverts, at home and abroad. Some girls didn't, but releasing nude or sexual images on the internet was something I couldn't imagine ever being comfortable with. I was also keen to keep my anonymity and to avoid being recognised. Only a few of my very closest friends knew about my work and I used several different aliases. I would often change name just to attract new customers and I rotated my profile pictures. Occasionally I would go with 'girl next door', other times I went for a more glamorous look.

After the move, I tried to live as normal a life as possible in Stockholm too. I did most of my work during the day, before heading out for the evening with friends, just like everybody else. Of course it was never easy, having to lie about what you did for a living, but that was a price I was willing to pay.

Just like my time abroad, I could pick and choose when I wanted to work. There was never any shortage of customers and I ended up with a few regulars there too. Many of them were pretty shy, almost afraid to touch me. As though I might crumble in front of them, and despite my ads being frank about what services I offered, they would still ask if this or that was okay. They always wanted to be on the safe side and to make 100 per cent sure that they weren't doing anything that would upset me.

After being back in Sweden a while I had attracted some wealthy regulars of my own, customers who would whisk me away on weekend breaks and all kinds of adventures, even if that sort of thing was nowhere near as regular as it had been in Australia. They always treated me like a princess.

One of the drawbacks of working in Stockholm as opposed to New York, Sydney or Miami was of course that the risk of being recognised was much greater. It did actually happen – but whenever I heard someone shouting one of my working names I would first pretend not to hear and then, quick as a flash, disappear into a crowd. The fact that it only happened a couple of times was naturally down to the customers being as keen to keep their meetings with me a secret as I was – paying for sex is illegal after all. And if they were married, or had kids, they were even more keen to be discreet, likewise if they were established in the upper echelons of society. If anyone asked, I used to say that I was a make-up artist and hope they wouldn't ask too many follow-up questions.

*

Time passed, and after a while I started pondering those big questions in life, as I think everyone does at a certain age. Was this the life for me? Was I happy? Didn't I long for real love? Until my thirtieth birthday arrived, I used to think that the day I was going to settle down with a man, a horse and a dog would arrive automatically, and that the best thing to do was to seize any opportunities to travel and just live my life while I was young and free. Now, though, I could feel my desire for a different life getting stronger and stronger. I noticed that I was actually getting bored of the partying, the travelling. All these superficial relationships, these short but intense meetings with new people, all the things I used to think were fun and exciting ... Now I was looking for something deeper, to give my existence meaning – a new life. I wanted a lasting relationship, not something that was only going to last weeks or months. Perhaps even something that would last forever.

Then, in mid-2014 I did meet someone. He was a carpenter and I fell head over heels in love. After a while, those initial feelings cooled off, without really being replaced by a deeper love. Not only that, he started showing more and more less appealing traits, and as he changed, so too did my feelings towards him. Of course there were ups and downs, as with any relationship. He lived in Uddevalla, so I spent a lot of time there, but when autumn came around my thoughts turned to Stockholm and the idea of going back to work there.

After a major row, I made up my mind. It wasn't worth missing out on all that money just for his sake. I told my boyfriend that I was a make-up artist, but apparently our relationship was serious enough for that not to feel good. I missed him, and the fact that I was going behind his back and lying to him was making me feel guilty. So, every Thursday evening I'd jump on a train back to Uddevalla so that I could spend the weekend there with him. I did slowly start to hope that maybe we were meant to be, and after a while I stopped escorting in Stockholm altogether. Almost straight away, though, our relationship was back in stormy waters. Deep down, I knew that I wasn't going to be able to take an ordinary job, so I lived off my savings while I contemplated whether or not we had a future together. It was an incredibly tough time.

By the end, I was spending most of my time just slouching around at his place, waiting for him to come home from work. His house was lovely, right on the coast, with lots of walks on the doorstep. Somewhere inside me was that desire to settle down, with a husband, a horse and a dog. My parents had a little dwarf poodle named Dolly when I was a kid and that was the kind of dog I'd always pictured whenever I imagined my own personal 'happy ever after'. So, in March 2015, I bought Nellie, an adorable toy poodle. Now I had two out of three – the 'husband' and the dog – yet I still wasn't really happy. We were together for ten months and I really don't know what it was that kept me umming and ahhing over him. Maybe it was just that I so wanted it to work.

As summer approached, my friend Nathalie asked whether we were going to America again, like we had the year before, and that really got me thinking. My boyfriend didn't say he thought I should go, but he didn't say I should stay either. It really felt like he didn't care, so that decision made itself.

The day after midsummer, just before Nathalie and I were due to leave, I split with my boyfriend. It turned out to be a good call. Me and Nathalie had a great holiday and, not only that, my old dream about studying in the States was re-awoken. After all, I was thirty and I couldn't go on being an escort forever.

That was that, I thought to myself. I was going to begin studying in America, then start my own business, meet and marry my soulmate and then live there for the rest of my days.

I made contact with several companies who specialised in arranging study abroad and they helped me apply to a number of colleges. I found one in Los Angeles that seemed really good, one that I could apply to despite not having good grades from school. Not only that, I already had a friend in LA, a Swede who was working as a model out there. She had loads of exciting contacts. Those could be the foundations of my new life – studying there, hanging out with her. I got really excited at the thought of moving, even before I knew whether or not I'd been accepted. I sat an obligatory English exam, which I passed with ease. I had only had a few clients over the previous months and escorting was definitely not something I missed. Now my life was heading in a whole new direction. One that was exciting, and one that gave me hope for the future. I was just going to see a few last customers. After that, I'd decided, I would be stopping for good.

Chapter Eight

FRIDAY

INTERROGATING OFFICER: *How did you imagine the day you released Isabel might pan out?*

MARTIN TRENNEBORG: *Do you mean …?*

INTERROGATING OFFICER: *After she had been locked up for several years. I mean, if she had ended up being locked up for years, which was always your intention. What were you planning to do then?*

MARTIN TRENNEBORG: *Hang myself.*

INTERROGATING OFFICER: *Hang yourself?*

MARTIN TRENNEBORG: *That's right.*

EXCERPT FROM INTERVIEW WITH
MARTIN TRENNEBORG

I wake up with no idea what time it is, and no way of finding out. I wish Martin had at least put in a slit window, just a sliver of daylight telling me whether it was night or day would have made my existence that little bit more bearable. I try to work out whether I feel like I've had enough sleep – that is usually anything over six hours. Now, though, it's impossible to tell. The tiredness that I've felt since day one in here is really something else. No matter what I do though, I can't get back to sleep, my thoughts are racing. I wonder how it's gone, whether Martin has managed to collect my stuff and is now on his way back, or whether he's been caught. He might even have died in a car crash. With that black thought twisting my insides I get out of bed to try to make some breakfast, anything to distract myself.

Nellie makes a little noise; I jump out of my skin and drop the butter knife onto the floor. I wheedle the nails out of the plank in the room next door, pop them in my pocket and then get down to my exercise routine: planking, sit-ups, push-ups, running on the spot. I need to make sure I stay as fit as I can. If the monster's plan succeeds, if he ends up making it back without anyone noticing him, then I am going to kill him.

At what feels like about two in the afternoon, I hear the first door slam shut. Without really knowing why, I sit down on the bed with my hands in my lap and take a deep breath. Perhaps I'm trying to look as innocent as possible. My thoughts are all over the place – today might be the day I kill, or it could be the day I get killed. My heart is pounding so quickly now that I feel dizzy and I'm so tense, so anxious to find out whether he's brought the bag or not, that I want to throw up. I mustn't give off any signals that suggest I might be planning to kill him. If I'm going to have any chance at all, I need to make sure it looks like my attitude hasn't changed. I need him to let his guard down and that will only happen if he trusts me.

I try to hide the fact that I'm looking behind him as he walks through the door, straining to see whether he's brought my big suitcase. My heart misses a beat. No suitcase. He is carrying a small green rucksack in one hand – has he only brought a few things? He doesn't say a word as he comes in, just plonks the bag down on the floor between us. Then he drags the two chairs over so that they're facing each other, sits on one himself and asks me to sit down on the other. I do as he says. His facial expressions are impossible to decode and eventually I just can't hold it in anymore: 'So, didn't you pick up my things?'

He clears his throat. Seems fairly calm, which makes me a little bit less tense. Then he says: 'Nope.' His eyes look different – *what is it now?* I can't help but mention my imprisonment, as I do every day, and I ask him about letting me go.

'Are you still planning to keep me here for a couple of years?'

He rubs his hand down his face. 'Nope.'

I don't know whether to be pleased or terrified by that. Does he mean that he's about to let me go, or that he's got tired of the whole thing and he's going to kill me?

Not without a fight, I think to myself.

Martin leans forward and pulls something out of the green bag. My heart rate slows slightly when I see that it's not some kind of weapon – it's an envelope. I gasp, then hold my breath. The envelope is clearly addressed to Isabel Eriksson, but the thing that seems to make time stand still is the Police logo in the top corner.

Martin opens the envelope and reaches inside it. 'It was taped to your front door,' he says, pulling out a note. 'It says that you've been reported missing. And I couldn't get into your flat because the police have changed the locks.'

He hands me the note. I am in shock and my heart is racing even faster still.

Isabel. Your loved ones are worried about you. They miss you and have reported you as a missing person.

My head is spinning, but I'm still vaguely aware of Martin's presence as he observes me very closely. Simply reading those words – getting a message from another human being after six days of having no contact with anyone except the psychopath who brought me here – brings tears to my eyes. My brain immediately swaps the words 'loved ones' for 'Mum' and 'Sis'. They're worried; they miss me. They have realised that something must be wrong and gone to the police.

There's still hope for me yet. Isn't there?

Martin reaches into the bag again and rummages around, still not saying anything. I am clutching the note from the outside world so tightly that my fingers hurt. Then my mouth falls open in sheer surprise. He pulls my driving licence and my phone out of the bag.

What's going on?

After that, he fishes out a door key and a car key.

What's he up to?

He then throws all of it onto the bed. The urge to grab my phone and ring 999 feels like a fire blazing under the surface of my skin. My hands are trembling and the note I'm holding starts to shake, but I daren't move or say anything. So when Martin then pulls out a pistol, I finally break down. I start crying uncontrollably and my whole body is shaking so much that I struggle to breathe. For a few awful seconds, I'm convinced he's about to shoot me and the dread rips through my insides. Throughout my panic attack, he just looks at me calmly, quite composed. Eventually I manage to get the tears under control even if my pulse is still racing wildly.

'Are you going to shoot me?' I blurt out before I have the chance to stop it, without knowing whether I want to hear his reply. There's nothing I can do. I dry my tears with the back of my hand, just hoping that he's not about to shoot me there and then, now that the police seem to be looking for me. *Is keeping me here too risky now?*

He smacks his lips and, after what seems like an eternity, he puts the pistol down next to me on the bed and says: 'Shoot me now and drive away. Take the car.' He nods towards the keys.

Dare I trust him? How can I, after everything he's done to me? If I do pick up the gun – even if it's just to make myself feel a bit safer – how do I know he's not going to kill me for it? How do I know that this isn't yet another one of his sick tests, now he knows that people are looking for me? The keys next to me might not even be the keys to the door out of here, or to his car. This might just be yet another game to him. If I pick the gun up, I'll get killed; if I don't, he'll let me go. Or he could be thinking the exact opposite. I really don't know. But what if ... what if he does let me just drive away?

Two of the doors have code locks and he hasn't given you the codes. There's your answer!

I sit there, helpless, trying not to let the hysteria take control of me altogether. And my mobile is lying there the whole time, screaming at me to pick it up and call 999. A darker voice is telling me to pick up the gun and pull the trigger. I can now call for help, even if he's dead. But I can't escape the memory of last time – I won't be able to do it. Besides, I don't even know if I'll be able to get a phone signal inside this bunker. After sitting there for a while, deep in my own thoughts, I see how Martin sighs and slumps back in his chair.

'I couldn't get into your flat,' he says again, gesturing towards the note in my hand.

I read it over and over again. There's a number at the bottom and it says to call if I want to get hold of the new keys or if I have any questions.

'I just grabbed the note and left. I went for a walk in Tessinparken, just wandered around for a while. Thinking ... and ... that's when I realised what I needed to do with you.'

I hold my breath.

'Keeping you locked up here … it's not a good idea.'

What the hell does that mean?

He grabs the pistol so suddenly that it makes me scream. Now my body is really shaking and my heartbeat is off the scale. Nellie jumps up onto the bed and starts barking like a mad thing and in my mind's eye I can see Martin shooting her first, then me.

'No!' I scream, much louder than I meant to. She wets herself, right there on the bed. *That might annoy him*, I think to myself, *he's been calm up to now*. As softly as I can, I explain that she hasn't been outside for ages, that that's why it's happened, that she would never normally do it. Wave upon wave of panic smashes into me; I can't take my eyes off the gun.

'Here's the key to get out,' he says patiently, as if talking to a child. 'And this –' he places the pistol in my lap. I shudder as I feel its ominous weight on my thigh. 'It's loaded, all you have to do is pull the trigger.'

Don't fall for it!

All my internal alarm bells are thundering away. But what if I ignore the gun, just pick up the phone and keys and walk away?

Might he shoot me in the back? Would he feel slighted if I – despite all my kind words – want to leave, just like all those other girls? All the options feel fraught with danger.

'I …' My voice cracks into a falsetto and then fades completely, so I take a deep breath and try again. 'I can't shoot you.'

Martin sighs. 'It would be considered self-defence. Chances are the police would give you a pat on the back for shooting me. Considering everything I've done … I deserve it.' But the lack of emotion is chilling. Is that really how you'd behave if you were seriously asking someone to shoot you?

Is this really happening? Is it a trick? Or is he really regretting it? Am I going to walk free today?

My desire to leave this dark, dusty prison is so strong that every hair on my body stands on end.

'D-does that … let me out?' I say, finally, pointing to the key next to me.

'It opens all the doors. If you've got that one, you don't need the codes.' His eyes are fixed on me as he says it, almost like he's studying me now. 'If you really can't kill me then shoot me in the kneecap. Then you can lock me in, take the car and go.'

I shake my head – I daren't do anything else. Martin looks at me, slowly stroking his hands along his thighs while he seems to be thinking.

'I can't face being in prison, I would rather take my own life,' he says.

That comment strikes fear into me again. Obviously he thinks I'll go to the police if he lets me free. That just leaves him with two choices: to keep me here, or to kill me. He goes on: 'Do you know what they do to sex offenders in prison?'

Pretty much what you're planning to do to me twice a day for a couple of years.

I say nothing though.

'I'll get beaten up all the time, or raped. I'd rather die.'

I wait to see what's coming next.

'Suicide by cop, do you know what that means? If you ring the police and tell them what's going on then maybe they'll send loads of officers down here. Then I can just wave that thing about,' he points to the pistol. 'Then they'll shoot me.'

Eventually I manage to get my mouth working. 'I'll tell them anything, whatever you want, if you just let us go. It doesn't have to be that way – you don't need to die, no one needs to die. You can tell me exactly what to say to the police and I'll do it. I wouldn't even need to mention your name. I can just say I went off somewhere. Please, just let us go. I don't want anyone to get hurt. Not you, not me. I just want to get out of here.'

He nods a couple of times. Then he slaps his hand on his thigh.

'I'll drive you to Stockholm.'

Suddenly it's as if my hysteria has been let loose – the words are just pouring out of me, through the tears. 'Thank God! Thank the good Lord! I've been praying, every day, an awful lot. I have thought long and hard about my life and I am going to change it if you let me go. Is this really happening? My God, this is a miracle!'

The smile that spreads across Martin's face shuts me up. I can't do anything about the sobbing though. He sits there, in silence, studying me. I wipe the tears and the snot from my face. Has it all been another cruel joke? With anyone else, you would think, *No one would go that far*, but, given this man has spent five years building a prison bunker, only one thing is certain: there are no lengths to which he's not prepared to go. My teeth are chattering now and the panic has come back with a vengeance. *Have I been getting ahead of myself? Is he playing games with me?* I sniffle weakly before I finally quieten down. I can feel how pathetic the pleading looks I'm giving Martin are, but I can't even manage to get upset about it – the fact that he's made me so submissive and so scared. I have run out of strength. Of determination. I'm just a shell. Broken. All I want is to get out of here.

'So,' Martin says as if he is about to have a chat about the weather, 'we should get going, if we're going to get there at a reasonable hour.'

These drastic, sudden changes of mood are what keep me feeling so on edge. Only a few minutes have passed since he was asking me to shoot him. Telling me how he planned to take his own life by waving a gun at the police. Now, though, he's acting like a normal human being. He looks almost happy. I find it terrifying, but I mustn't let it show. I need to keep trying to believe that somehow, deep in his madness, he is mad enough to let me go in the belief that he'll get away with everything. That he'll be able to simply put it behind him as if nothing has happened.

'Right, okay? So ... let's go then?' I reply cautiously, trying to hurry him along before he changes his mind, and I look around inside the bunker. There's nothing to pack. Everything I have here is lying next to me on the bed.

Then Martin picks up the gun again. My eyes open wide. *No!*

'Calm down,' he says. 'To make sure you feel safe, you can have this. You can just pull the trigger, whenever you like, if you don't trust me.' He passes me the pistol and the green bag and tells me to stand up. I am absolutely terrified, fearing for my life. I just can't shake the feeling that all of this might be a fucked-up, evil test. But then as he heads for the door I hurry after him, quietly thanking God for hearing my prayers, while carefully placing the weapon in the green rucksack. I call Nellie over; I pick her up and hold her to my chest. Suddenly I notice my Louis Vuitton handbag is lying there beside the door – I was planning to take it to that dinner we were supposed to be going to. Just seeing something of mine, something from the world outside, sets my bottom lip quivering again. Without a word, Martin picks it up and hands it to me.

Is this real? Is the miracle about to happen?

I check the contents of the bag: keys, lipgloss, old receipts and some cash. I pop my driving licence and my phone in too.

'You said you'd been thinking a lot about your life,' Martin says, unlocking the first of the doors.

'Yes,' I say. I'm just behind him, practically bouncing on the spot, desperate to get out of the bunker.

'What did you think about?'

I tell him that I plan to stop working as an escort and to spend more time with my family. Make my dreams a reality, now that God has given me another chance; how I have realised what really matters in life. Martin opens the second door.

'That sounds great,' he says.

I hold the rucksack out in front of me, constantly aware of the pistol inside and the fact that – according to Martin – it's loaded. Imagine if it goes off? I'm terrified and I ask him if it's safe to have it in there like that.

'Don't worry,' is all he says in reply. Slowly we approach the third door: him first, me, with Nellie in my arms, right behind him.

Here we go, I think to myself. *This is where it turns out to be a cruel joke, or maybe a test. If he does lock me up again after this it really will crush me completely.*

Then we're outside and he still hasn't changed his mind and I can hardly believe it. I can see sunlight, feel the rays on my cheeks and squint towards it. I fill my lungs with the fresh woodland air and study the beautiful trees around me. I'm struck by the deep-green beauty and the birdsong is almost deafening. Martin, though, isn't walking towards the car, which is parked a few metres away: he is heading straight for his house.

Never mind what he's up to. Run. Just run for your life! You're out, Nellie's in your arms and you're not chained to him.

My legs twitch, but I daren't run. How do I know whether or not he's got more weapons? I do stop though, and Martin notices and turns round straight away.

'I'm just going to pack a few things,' he says, seeing my hesitation. 'You can sit on the steps and wait for me, if you like. Put the dog down, I'm sure she'll want to run around a bit.'

My trembling arms lower Nellie to the ground. She goes berserk when she realises that she's being allowed to run free. She darts off and around in a loop, barking and jumping as though she's never been outside before in her life. The scene brings a tear to my eye.

Martin looks a bit unsure. He stops and looks at me intently. 'When we get to Stockholm, you *can* tell people the truth. That you've been ... my prisoner. But in that case you might as well just get the gun out and shoot me right here and now.'

I shake my head. 'I won't say anything, I promise.'

That seems to satisfy him and he heads into the house. I perch on the steps leading up to the front door. Then I look up at the sky and say another prayer: that this is it; that today's the day I will finally go free. Only a minute or so later, Martin emerges carrying a plastic bottle – mineral water. He hands it to me with the words: 'It's not spiked.'

I freeze halfway through my movement and then take it from him. This man has told me lie after lie since the moment we met; I cannot trust him. But I notice the security seal around the cap is intact so I open the bottle and take a few gulps. He heads back inside and I carefully put the bottle down next to me and do my best to breathe. After a few minutes he returns.

'We can go now.'

It takes a while to catch Nellie – she really is not keen. The poor creature probably thinks we're heading back into that filthy bunker. Eventually I do manage to grab her and head over to the car. Martin has told me that he's going to drive me to Stockholm and I daren't say anything at all about his plan in case it makes him change his mind. I sit myself down in the passenger seat.

'Would you like a blanket?'

'Yes, that would be great, thanks,' I say, and Nellie snuggles down on my lap. My heart is pounding away. It might not sound like a very long time, but six days and nights is a long time to spend locked up in a confined space with no light, no fresh air, no contact with anyone except the psychopath who has brought you there, and now everything feels a bit surreal. I jump, startled by the engine revving into life. As we slowly pull away Martin tells me what *he* thinks I should say to people when I get back: 'They are going to wonder, you know.'

He tells me to say that we met on the Saturday. That we had such a great time that we decided I should go back with him, so that he could go to work on Monday without us having to part. I'm to say that I didn't have a charger with me, that my battery went, and that's why no one's been able to get hold of me. Then that he has brought me back today, Friday, and that we didn't have a clue that people were worried or had reported me missing.

'It'll be best for both of us,' he says, 'because surely you don't want your family and friends knowing that you were working as an escort? If you do tell the truth, everyone's going to find out. First, the police, then your whole family.'

I peer out at the gravel track we're driving along – this really is the back of beyond. I feel a sharp anger at his words – his tone makes it sound like drugging and kidnapping a woman, holding her hostage for six days, is really no big deal.

You HOPE it'll be six days. You've no way of knowing. Could be more, you're not safe yet.

I look down at the rucksack between my feet and think about the pistol inside. It's still making me feel very uneasy and it feels like it could just go off at any minute. When I say as much to Martin he stops the car, jumps out, grabs the bag and then puts it in the boot.

'We can stop again whenever you like, if you decide you want it,' he says.

Then as we move off again I spot a house on the left-hand side. Further along, a sign – *Axeltorp* – and I tell myself to remember that name, so I can tell the police where I've been. That's if I do make it. I can tell them where this man – the one who did this to me and who might do it again, given the chance – lives.

'Axeltorp?' I say, still completely clueless as to our whereabouts.

I notice Martin's mouth turn up at the corners.

'Where are we?' I ask when he doesn't respond.

He seems to give it some thought, then he comes out with it: 'Skåne.'

Skåne? Six hundred kilometres from Stockholm? This means that he's transported me, a dead weight, all that way without anyone noticing anything. Even though it's comforting in a way to know where we are, it makes me feel chillingly alone.

'I think you ought to ring your mum, or someone – let them know you're okay,' Martin says as he pulls out onto a wider, tarmacked road. 'They were worried about you, according to that note. I can take you to Uddevalla if you prefer. If you think I'm playing games, you can jump out somewhere along the way. Wherever you like.' His tone is so off, as if we are old friends and nothing strange at all has happened between us. As though the last six days have simply been erased from history.

'But then all your stuff's in Stockholm,' he adds as an afterthought.

I think carefully about it. What I would really like to do is go home, to Uddevalla, but it's pretty obvious that he wants to take me to Stockholm. There's no way I'm calling someone and telling them I'm fine; I don't want to do that until I'm absolutely sure that I'm safe. Free of this man. Maybe that's all he's after – to trick me, get me to make that call and say that I'm okay. If I do, what's to say he won't just turn the car around and take me straight back to the bunker? Or just drive deep into the forest and murder me?

'Stockholm is great. I'll call as soon as we arrive,' I reply in as relaxed a voice as I can manage when everything inside of me is still churning violently.

*

Martin speaks almost incessantly for the entire journey and that makes me nervous. During my time as his captive he was rather quiet. Said whatever he said calmly and deliberately, nothing superfluous. In fact, it has been that creepily quiet manner of his that has terrified me so much and now his non-stop babbling is having the same effect, which makes me wonder whether he is actually losing his mind. Whether he's finally snapped. *What if he crashes the car on purpose? He seems tired anyway.* I hold Nellie tightly and will the car onwards, wishing it could go a bit faster, but as I get more and more concerned that he might crash I ask if maybe we should swap – if maybe I should drive. He says he thinks that's a good idea.

While I drive us northwards, he explains in detail again how he managed to abduct me. About the strawberries, and how the drugged ones were marked. About us having sex. I grip the wheel tightly throughout and my foot is getting heavier on the gas. I can see freedom, right in front of me, just a few hours away if I play my cards right. I do respond here and there but avoid any criticism, despite feeling quite sick as I listen to him proudly recounting the tale.

'I had a bottle of juice with me, which you drank, and there was flunitrazepam in that too.'

I tell him I don't remember: not the juice, nor us having sex.

He smiles. 'Obviously I took the condom with me when we left. You can't leave that kind of DNA print at the scene.'

I struggle to keep both the retching and the tears under control. *Focus on the driving. Driving away from the bunker. Towards other people.* Every metre I put between me and the bunker feels like another mini-victory.

'Weird,' he says suddenly, out of nowhere. 'That it took so much to get you under. I basically had to use everything I had with me. Same thing in the car. You came round once while we were driving – do you remember that?'

He makes it sound like we're reminiscing about our most recent motoring holiday together rather than when he kidnapped me. I nod, and the roadside signs tell me we're almost halfway to Stockholm.

'You asked me where you were.' He chuckles. 'I had to make something up. Then you were out again. I stopped for a break a couple of times and I checked your blood pressure. Lucky you, though – kidnapped by a doctor, eh? Who could make sure you were okay, I mean.'

I can barely take this in; I want to scream at the top of my lungs but I stifle it. Martin goes quiet for a few minutes and then changes tack again.

'How attractive do you think you are, on a scale of one to ten?'

Again, I'm stunned. I have no idea where this is going but it's perfectly clear that he does want an answer. *What does he want to hear?*

'I dunno. A seven, maybe?'

'Typical woman, playing yourself down like that. You're a fucking twelve!'

I take a deep breath. If nothing else, I'm very relieved not to be talking about the abduction anymore.

'What about me then?' he asks.

'Oh … I don't know …'

A fucking psychopath is what you are. If I go too low maybe he'll get angry.

'… a six?'

He contemplates that in silence for a moment as the world swishes past the window. Then he changes the subject yet again.

'I'm surprised you didn't shoot me.'

What the hell am I supposed to say to that? I can't think of anything, so I stay quiet.

He goes on: 'I really didn't think I'd be sitting here now. I can't believe … today. That you don't … well, that you didn't want … revenge. I think most people would have pulled the trigger. Killed or at least injured me. Because they'd have been so angry.'

'I'm not a violent person,' I blurt out. 'I could never hurt anyone.'

'This could be a fresh start for both of us.' He folds down the sunscreen on his side and inspects himself in the mirror, adjusting his hair as he talks. 'Maybe I should give online dating a go? And you need to stop the escorting. It's such a waste – a girl like you, who could do anything, doing that. And you choose not to have a proper relationship, I just can't believe it.'

I tell him that I think he should definitely try internet dating. That he's sure to find a girl to spend his life with.

I tell him that a good-looking doctor like him, charming to boot, has everything going for him. That lots of people who meet online end up getting married and having kids. I try to persuade him that he will find someone so that he doesn't suddenly decide to lock me in again. I also tell him that I am going to stop escorting and he smiles approvingly.

'You know what?' He stares at me for ages until I respond: 'No, what?'

'I really wasn't expecting you to be so kind – I thought you'd be a bit of a bitch. Like what you'd expect of an escort. If you had been like that, I probably never would've let you go.'

He slams the sunscreen back up quite forcefully and I jump in fright. I certainly don't feel like I've been 'let go', as he puts it. Not yet. I won't until I'm a long way away from Martin Trenneborg.

'If you had been a bitch, you would've deserved it.'

It suddenly feels like being in free fall. My body understands long before my conscious brain does. Understands that in my desperation, in choosing how to interact with my kidnapper, I made the right choice. I am so incredibly lucky that I went with the kind and submissive approach – it probably saved my life.

'Then there was that note too.'

'Note?' I say, my voice now barely a whisper.

'The one on the door saying your loved ones missed you. I don't think it had occurred to me that someone like you, well

... an escort, I mean, would be missed. Or have loved ones who cared about you.'

Before I manage to gather my thoughts and come up with a reply he points to a sign at the roadside: 'I'm hungry. Shall we take a break here, get ourselves a Burger King?'

Everything is telling me no, keep driving. As quickly as possible. All the way to Stockholm. No stopping. Don't give him any more time than you have to – what if he suddenly changes his mind? I can't say any of that of course, so I nod, indicate and we turn off.

*

It's Friday night, but the sun is still bright. Here I am, sitting in a Burger King somewhere between Skåne and Stockholm, staring at a burger meal on the table between me and my kidnapper. I can see his car through the window. What I really want to do is scream to everyone in here that they should save me, but what if he decides to get the pistol from the car and starts shooting in all directions? So I keep up the pretence. I try to memorise his number plate. Of course Martin might not even be his real name, he might be lying about that. If that's the case, I don't know how the police will ever find him, if I do get the chance to report this. To try to disguise the fact that I'm looking at the number plate, I ask him what the weather has been like in the week I've been locked up.

'Awful,' he says through a mouthful of cheeseburger. 'Autumn weather.'

I look around the restaurant. Couples, lone individuals and families. None of them has any idea that I'm sitting here with my kidnapper, still petrified that he's going to take me back to the bunker. All they see is a woman eating a hamburger.

'Where are you going to go, when we get to Stockholm?'

I consider my response carefully. 'To my friend Nathalie's place. I can stay there.'

'Don't you want to give her a call? Tell her you're on your way?'

'She's always at home at this time on a Friday. Probably getting ready to go out later.'

He thinks about it for a moment, then pulls out his own phone and dials a number. I listen intently, but it just rings a few times and then he hangs up.

'Who did you call?' I ask.

'My brother. He lives in Stockholm. I thought maybe I could sleep there. He didn't answer though, so I guess it's a hotel for me. Do you fancy it?'

I splutter. 'No, thanks. I'm good. I really want to sleep at Nathalie's.'

He looks disappointed.

*

With just a few dozen kilometres left to Stockholm Martin tells me to call the number on the note and ask where I can pick up the new keys to my apartment.

Something doesn't feel right. Is this his plan? Have me convince people I'm fine and make sure the missing person case is closed, then get the new keys before he finally takes me back to the bunker? I think he notices I'm thinking along those lines because after a while he says: 'Or you can just ring when we get to Stockholm. And by the way, I think we ought to stop in at your place and check nothing has changed.'

'How do you mean?'

I just want to get straight to the police.

'I mean, if we're going to stick to our ... story, plus it might be a bit suss if we haven't noticed a new note? That sort of thing?'

I notice that focusing on what he's saying is becoming a struggle. The traffic is getting heavier as we get closer to Stockholm, and I'm not really used to driving in cities. Despite all my instincts telling me not to stop unless we absolutely have to, I suggest we swap again – that he should drive the last few kilometres. He agrees, so we stop at a retail park on the outskirts of the city and swap places.

As we finally pull into the car park in front of my apartment block, the nerves are getting worse. I get the feeling he's going to try something; I don't know what. Martin says I can wait in the car while he goes up to check if there's a new note, but I want to see what he's doing. *The pistol is still in the boot, what if he goes to get it?* We both climb out. Nellie needs to wee but I daren't put her down, daren't take my eyes off Martin. He taps in the door code and steps inside. I follow him in.

This is weird. Emotional. Just a few hours ago, I didn't know whether I would ever get to see Stockholm or my temporary home again. I see a large yellow sign on my front door that says 'POLICE LINE DO NOT CROSS'. There's no new note though, so we walk back down to the car together. I pull the note from my bag. Martin instructs me to call the number, but when I do, there's no answer. The disappointment is heartbreaking, like a great black monster eating me up from the inside out.

'Hmm,' Martin says, muttering in his normal, collected way. 'They should be at the police station on Kungsholmen. We'll drive down there, get the keys, then I can bring you back here.'

Don't you believe it, I think to myself. *That could have been his plan all along: get the keys, show everyone I'm fine, get rid of any evidence from inside the apartment and then kidnap me again. Never to let me go.*

'N-no. There's no need. I'll get a taxi straight from there over to my friend's place.'

My plan, of course, is to tell the police exactly what has happened as soon as he's dropped me off, and to hope that he doesn't get too far before they can arrest him pretty much straight away.

When we get there, he pulls up on the opposite side of the street, where you're not supposed to stop, and looks me straight in the eye.

'Try that number again,' he says.

I do as he says, but again, no answer.

I've been expecting to jump out, and for Martin to drive off, finally setting me free. To my horror, he gets out too and walks towards the entrance with me.

'I don't expect this'll take long, what do you think?' he says.

Then we step through the doors and into the police station.

*

As I enter the police station, it's as if the exhaustion of the last few days suddenly washes over me. The terror, all the awful things I've been through, the constant despair, being drugged, being raped; the fear that I would never see my family again. Now it's as if the dark cloud above me has suddenly burst, letting the rain pour down. Maybe it's because I can see the ultimate symbol of safety and security right there in front of me – police uniforms – yet somehow still feel at the mercy of this crazy doctor. It could be the unbearable strain of keeping up the pretence throughout the six-hour journey: playing along and trying to keep up with his mood swings. Who knows? Right now though, it feels as though every cell in my body weighs several tons. And despite being surrounded by policemen I still can't let go. My brain starts imagining scenarios such as Martin running out to the car and grabbing the pistol before returning and shooting everyone. At first I try to shake it off by reminding myself that thinking like that is completely insane, but when I remember just what this man has done to me I realise nothing is impossible.

I approach the counter at reception. The policeman behind the desk is called Andreas, according to the name badge on his chest. What I really want to do now is scream out loud. I want to cry. It would be such a relief to finally feel free and let go of my fear; to be able to share it, and the rage. Martin is standing right next to me though, as if he wants to hear what I'm about to say.

I recall him telling me to be a bit annoyed when I ask for my keys. As though it was preposterous for someone to have reported me missing in the first place, and as though I'm furious that they've changed the locks because it's really put me out. So I do my best. I pull out the note and say: 'Apparently I've been reported missing, but I've just been staying with my friend here.' I gesture towards Martin. 'And you've changed the locks on my front door, so I can't get in. I would really like you to give me the keys.'

Andreas looks about my age, perhaps a year or two younger. He's well built. I stand there and hope that he can see in my eyes that there's really rather more to it than what I've told him. Hope he notices that something's not right.

'Okay, could I see some ID, please?' he replies.

I pull out my driving licence and I hope, dearly, that he's about to ask Martin too. That way, they'll know exactly who he is. I do my best to cry for help using only my eyes; a cry that Martin must not see. Andreas, though, says only: 'Just bear with me a second, I'll see if I can find any keys.'

He walks off, leaving the two of us standing there in reception. Me and my abductor. At the police station.

Andreas comes back.

'You've been reported missing, possibly kidnapped. Plenty of resources have been put into this, into trying to find you. Take a seat, you can talk to one of the officers on the case.' He points us in the direction of a couple of chairs.

Once again, my heart is racing. This wasn't part of the plan. I glance over at Martin. *Possibly kidnapped.* Might that scare him? Make him angry? I don't know what sort of thing might cause him to flip out, but my talking to one of the officers on the case can hardly be a dream scenario for him. Slowly, very slowly, I sit down on one of the chairs and Martin sits down next to me. Throughout all this, I can't understand why the police aren't reacting differently. I mean, I've been reported missing, a suspected abduction. Now here I am, walking into a police station accompanied by a man who hasn't said a word. I'm wearing clothes that are far too big for me and are obviously not my own. Not only that, they're dusty and dirty. I know how bad I look. Worn out, with massive bags under my eyes – I haven't slept properly in almost a week. How could they *not* see that something was wrong? I try to make eye contact with police officers as they walk past, but we're just left sitting there, me and Martin, and I'm getting more and more terrified with each second that passes. If he really is planning to let me go, why doesn't he just leave? Why is he still watching me like this?

Martin leans over to me and starts showing me pictures from his Facebook page. Him on a climbing trip ... Pictures he's taken of nurses he thinks are pretty ... Then he shows me a picture of himself with a girl and tells me they used to see each other.

'What do you think? She's gorgeous, isn't she?'

I just nod.

'That's a shemale,' he whispers. 'She was going to be your roommate.'

I gulp as I try not to cry. I don't want to ruin everything now, not when I'm so close to being saved. I nod again and pretend to adjust the bottom of my trousers while I quickly dry my tears.

'The pistol,' he whispers and I freeze. 'It's almost exactly like the ones the police use.'

Quite instinctively, I look over towards the policemen behind the desk, hoping they heard what's just been said, but they seem unmoved. Chatting away. Shuffling paper. Joking and laughing. *If they only knew what was going on right before their eyes*, I think to myself, and it's all I can do to stop myself from screaming out loud.

We wait and wait and wait, Martin trying small talk, me giving one-word answers. I'm still attempting to make eye contact with passing officers: I want them to see me, and to understand. I daren't stare too long though, in case Martin notices. Finally, after almost two hours, another policeman appears and he seems to be heading towards me. He opens the door to a little interview room and waves me over.

'Isabel? This way, please.'

I'm shaking so much that I can barely get to my feet, but in the end I do manage. When I notice Martin stand up and turn to follow, I almost throw up.

'We just want to speak to Isabel,' the officer says.

I turn around and see Martin hesitate. Then he says, as lightly as he can manage – by this point I know him well enough to tell when he's acting – 'Okay, I'll wait here then.'

It's when I'm about three paces away that the officer probably notices that something is very wrong. I have my back to Martin, who is now several metres away, and heading towards a waiting policeman. I can't hold back the tears any longer, but I bite down hard on my lip to keep quiet. I try to keep my back as straight as I can, try not to give anything away to the psychopath sitting behind me. I can feel his stare like daggers in my back. The policeman's eyes widen as he sees the tears rolling down my face but, thank God, he doesn't say a word.

Two steps left. I think I'm going to faint. Or else wake up and realise that I'm back in the bunker and this was all just a dream. The policeman frowns and looks a bit puzzled.

One step. Once I enter the little room and the door swings shut behind me, I let it all go. I break down, stumble; I almost fall to the floor. I have to prop myself up against the table and now my whole body is shaking violently; I'm crying hysterically and I'm struggling to breathe. It feels as though every last drop of air has been squeezed from my lungs.

The policeman, who had been about to sit down, rushes over and grabs hold of me.

'Can he ... can I be heard through the door?'

I can tell that the penny is finally beginning to drop.

'No,' the officer replies. 'He can't hear. What's been going on?'

'I need ... I have ... he ...' I stumble on every word. Then, after taking a few deep breaths, I manage to blurt out what I've been dying to say since last Saturday. 'I've been kidnapped. The man sitting out there kidnapped me. He has a pistol in the boot of his car, a black Volvo V70, parked outside. The number plate ends in 707.' I try to shake off a little spasm but end up collapsing onto one of the chairs.

'You ... what? Calm down, nice and slow. Can you say that again?'

'Can he get in here?'

'No, you're safe here.'

I try to speak more clearly; repeat what I've just said. Now he understands. He really understands and he wastes no time in acting.

'Wait here,' he says and opens another door. Then he leaves me alone in the little interview room. I try to get my breathing under control: deep breaths, while clutching Nellie to my chest. I can hardly believe that this is really happening.

'We made it, poppet. We're free,' I sniffle and kiss the top of her head. But I'm still straining to hear anything from out there, expecting to hear gunshots at any moment. *Am I really safe here?* Through a small pane at the top of the door, I see four policemen rush past, talking urgently as they go. Four. *That must mean they're going to arrest him, right?* I tug at the arms of the t-shirt, rub my eyes, shift around on the chair. I don't know what to do with myself; I don't even know what to feel. It's all just too much and slowly I begin to truly understand the scale of what I've been through; how it could've ended. I am so lucky to be sitting here now, yet I can't help still being scared. I didn't do what Martin said – I didn't stick to his plan about what to say. *What if they don't believe me and they let him go? What if he manages to escape? Would he track me down, desperate for revenge? He knows where I live. Knows where my mum lives.* The stubborn fear in my chest is going nowhere.

I'm so sick of being afraid.

After a while, the officer comes back. He stops just inside the door and he's looking at me quite differently now. Noticing my clothes. The state I'm in. And his eyes fill with compassion. At least *he* believes me, that much is certain.

'We found the weapon in the boot, just as you said,' he says as he sits down. 'We have arrested him, you don't need to be afraid anymore.' He clasps his hands on the table. 'So. Can you tell me everything? From the beginning.'

Only now do I dare to believe that the nightmare might finally be over. I lift Nellie up towards me again. She licks the tears from my cheeks and now I'm smiling and sobbing at the same time.

'We made it, poppet. We survived,' I whisper in her ear.

Chapter Nine

THE AFTERMATH

We were not completely free though, and perhaps we never will be. The interview at the police station went on for hours and I think it must have been one in the morning before we finished. The policeman conducting the interview interrupted me several times to ask me to repeat things, worried he might have heard wrong as I told him everything that Martin had said and done. It was plain to see that he could hardly believe what he was hearing. In fact, I can hardly believe it myself.

Straight after the first interview I was taken to SÖS, the main hospital located in the Södermalm district of Stockholm. It also hosts a special emergency clinic for the victims of rape. Unfortunately Nellie wasn't allowed to come along, so the police agreed to look after her for the night. Leaving her felt like I was leaving part of myself behind. We had got through it all together and I'm not sure what might have happened if she hadn't been there with me.

At the hospital, I had to re-tell the whole story again. Then I asked to borrow a phone. I couldn't get mine to work – no matter how hard I tried, I just couldn't remember the PIN. I just couldn't wait anymore: I had to call my mum. It was the middle of the night and I wasn't even sure whether she'd pick up the phone. As it rang, the tears poured down my face again. She did answer, a crackly, sleepy, 'Hello?'

'Mum ...' my voice cracked again. 'It's me.'

She screamed. 'Isabel! What happened? Where are you?'

As briefly as I could, I explained that I was safe, in hospital. Mum was in tears, explaining how terribly worried they'd been. How they'd thought I was dead. She also said I should call Nathalie.

'She's been in constant touch with the police, really trying to get them to keep things moving.'

After more tears, we hung up. Then I called Nathalie, but there was no answer.

The nurse returned as I was putting the phone down and asked me to get undressed. They took photos of the bruises and marks on my body and then did a gynaecological examination. As I'd suspected, I had developed thrush, so they started treating that immediately. I was told they'd be keeping me in overnight. Part of me just wanted to get home, but in a way it felt good not being alone. I was given a room on my own and the kind nurse told me just to press the buzzer if I got scared, or if I needed anything, and that she'd be straight there. She took my hand in hers.

'I can sit in this chair next to the bed until you fall asleep, if you like. And remember: you're free now. You can come and go as you please.'

I thanked her and told her I'd be okay. As soon as she was out the door, I rushed into the shower. Soon I was scrubbing away as though I could scrape off the whole awful experience. Just ripping off the clothes that belonged to my kidnapper made me feel thousands of kilos lighter. I would never have expected to be so pleased to be able to pull on the hospital gown. By the time I'd finished, it was 4am. My thoughts just refused to stop racing and, despite being completely whacked, I just couldn't settle down. I was going to be getting up early the next morning to talk to the special investigators and I was badly in need of a few hours' sleep. Despite all of that, I just could not sleep. After a while there was a knock at the door – the friendly nurse popped her head in.

'I made you a little sandwich. Thought you might be hungry?'

She had also brought a sleeping tablet and, even after I'd taken it, I still struggled to fall asleep. My heart was pounding and I was struggling to come to terms with the fact that I wasn't in the bunker anymore. That the footsteps I could hear outside the door didn't belong to my captor. I just kept staring at the painted walls and the door, which I wanted left slightly open. I must have fallen asleep eventually because the next thing I knew it was eight thirty and I was being woken by another wonderful nurse bringing me breakfast. I had another go at remembering the PIN on my phone – and it worked! The first call I made was to a lawyer friend of mine.

'Christ, I'm just so happy to hear your voice! I thought you were dead, we all did,' he said when he realised who he was speaking to.

So did I, I think to myself. *So did I.*

*

The next few days were full of interview after interview. Each new police officer I met said the same thing: that they'd never even heard of anything like this, at least not in Sweden. Everybody mentioned Josef Fritzl. Watching their reactions actually helped me to take in what I'd been through, made me realise what grave danger I had been in, got me to see what a dangerous man Martin Trenneborg really is.

On the Monday I got an email from Facebook's user support, confirming that they had approved my new login details. I didn't know what it was about at first, but it dawned on me as I read backwards in the email conversation. Martin had taken a photo of my driving licence and sent it to Facebook. Claiming to be me, he had told them that I'd forgotten my username and password and that I needed new ones so this was to confirm that Facebook had approved them. I was so lucky that the email hadn't arrived earlier – if he had got access to my Facebook account while I was in the bunker he'd have been able to tell everyone that I was fine, perhaps that I'd gone to Australia or something, so the case would have been closed and no one would have been looking for me. They would never have changed the locks on my apartment and so Martin could have picked up my stuff as planned. And then I might still be sitting in that dusty, terrifying bunker.

It turned out that I had an awful lot to thank Nathalie for. She'd called twice on that Saturday, and then she'd sent a text, but she never got a reply. Later on she noticed that I hadn't logged in to Facebook for some time so she sent a message there too: *Where are you sweetie? Get in touch, I'm starting to get a bit worried!! See you tomorrow <3*

We had talked about meeting up on Sunday; the day turned out to be my first in the bunker. When she woke up to find that I hadn't responded to any of her messages, and still hadn't logged in, she tried to call me several times, but my phone was switched off. In the hours that followed she tried whatever she could think of to get hold of me and she kept trying to tell herself that I was a very spontaneous person, that perhaps I'd just headed off somewhere and forgotten my charger; that I must have lost my phone, or perhaps had it nicked. By Monday, though, she was sure something was wrong. She got hold of a friend of mine back in Uddevalla and asked if I'd been in touch – I hadn't, of course. The next day she went over to my place, while my mum called the police. Nathalie hammered on the door, screamed through the letterbox and rattled the door handle. When the police arrived, they were very reluctant to force their way in. Most people who go missing do so of their own free will, they said. They nearly always come back and cases of young women disappearing against their will are almost unheard of. They did their best to calm Nathalie down, but she was convinced something had happened to me. She wouldn't leave the police alone, nagging and prodding them and telling them there was no way I would ever just disappear like that. In the end, they did kick the door down and Nathalie marched in, even though they'd told her to wait outside. Straight away, she noticed that the bedclothes were missing but nothing else had been taken. That left her in no doubt that something was very wrong. After that she stayed in daily contact with them – maybe her persistence helped to sharpen minds and meant they gave my case a bit more attention than they would have otherwise. I am so incredibly lucky to have a friend like her. It was very fortunate that I was reported missing so early – by Tuesday morning – so that the locks had been changed by the time Martin went back to collect my stuff.

After the second day of interviews, we decided that Nellie and I would stay at her place and, for the first time since the whole thing started, we got a decent night's sleep.

Thank you, Nathalie. From the bottom of my heart.

Chapter Ten

THE NIGHTMARE

I find myself inside a large house. I don't know where I am, but it's not Sweden – it's hot. I'm on the first floor. Suddenly, I hear a voice from downstairs. A man. I listen intently, and as I slowly recognise the voice, I can feel the panic rush in. *Can that really be Martin? Yes, it really is.*

I knew this might happen, that he could come back, but I never believed that it would happen. The panic grabs hold of me immediately; the one thing I fear above all else has come true. There's a little window in the room – I peer out and it's a long way down. If I jump, I might die or break my legs. Now I hear footsteps coming up the stairs; they're getting closer and closer. Without stopping to think, I jump. *Anything is better than being back in his clutches.* When I hit the ground though, I'm not outside but back in the room – standing eyeball-to-eyeball with the psychopath. He's carrying a long plank, his eyes are filled with rage and he says: 'I'm going to fucking kill you!'

Then we're on the sofa, in the living room, sitting next to each other. He has put the plank down and I just can't believe this is happening – my worst nightmare, all over again. I didn't think he would come after me, didn't think he'd be looking for revenge, but I was wrong. This time, I'm not going to make it. This time, he's going to torture and then murder me.

'What was it like, inside?' I ask nervously.

He turns towards me. I notice that he's wearing a sweatband, one with the words *Marry Me* scrawled across his forehead. He is calm and collected, but the look in his eyes is that of a madman.

'I've been working out,' he says before sitting down on a chair opposite me. He starts tapping me lightly with the plank, watching how I react – he does it to show me who's in charge. The blows get harder and I know that he's planning to bludgeon me to death. That's my punishment, for telling the police the truth. When the next wave of panic rolls in I wake to find Nellie lying next to me and whining.

The initial relief feels like drinking a glass of iced water on a really hot day. After that come the tears and the fear and I curl up into a ball. I have talked about this with my family, my friends and the police: this fear that he is going to look for revenge. That he will be back. Everyone tells me how very unlikely that is, but it makes no difference. I know the freakiest, most unlikely things can happen when you least expect them. *Will I ever be free again?*

*

Later that same day, I pull myself together and head out for a walk with Nathalie and Nellie. The next shock hits me as we're passing a newsstand. Every single headline is about me, all the front pages: *Doctor Takes Woman Prisoner.* I rush home and turn on my computer. All of the Swedish newspapers are reporting this, as well as sites from around the world. That's when I realise this is far from over; that the nightmare is not yet at an end.

Chapter Eleven
THE TRIAL

Day one of the trial, and I am incredibly nervous. I have no idea what to expect.

I have already met the prosecutor for a preliminary hearing. They told me about some of what Martin had told them during his interviews – for example, his account of what had actually been going on when he came in with the pistol and asked me to shoot him. I'm given a short excerpt to read:

'Do you know what a litmus test is?'

'What do you mean?' asks the officer.

'No, of course. If you don't know anything about chemistry ... It's a little strip of paper which you can dip in liquids to find out whether they are acidic or alkaline. You measure the pH. Are you with me? Let's say you have a weapon, but it's not real. The other person doesn't know that, though. It can be a ... let's see ... a great way to find out about the other person's true intentions, right? A sure-fire way to find out whether they would hurt you, given the chance. If the other

*person does pull the trigger nothing happens, but you do find
out. That is real power.'*

'So it wasn't real?' asks the officer.

'Of course not,' says Martin. 'As I said, litmus.'

Reading those words chills me to the bone and once again the
tears are welling up. What he was saying gradually dawns on
me: it *was* a test. What would have happened if I'd actually
tried to shoot him, right there in the bunker? If I had 'failed'
the test? Would I still be locked up in there? He did say one of
the reasons he was letting me go was that I was so kind – and
that he hadn't expected me to be.

The story has been all over the press, all around the world,
and since it broke I have had newspapers, TV reporters and
news websites after me. Day after day, the media is full of
images from inside the bunker, reports of fresh details that
journalists have unearthed. For a few weeks, the whole world
is talking about 'The Swedish Fritzl' and people don't seem to
be able to get enough of everything I've been through. As well
as trying to cope with all that, I am preparing myself for the
trial, with the help of my lawyer, and talking to a psychologist
to begin to work through the trauma. Every time I pass a
newsstand, I see Martin Trenneborg's face staring out at me,
or pictures of the bunker, or the farm, and each time I am
totally winded by it.

I feel vulnerable to say the least as I head for the courtroom,
wearing a headscarf and large dark glasses. I've found out
that Martin will admit his guilt, which is welcome news,

but only to the charges relating to the kidnapping and the imprisonment. Despite telling me about it several times, he now denies having had sex with me while I was drugged. His lawyer argues that the charge should be the less serious 'false imprisonment'.

My own lawyer and I enter the courtroom via a side entrance, so that I don't have to battle through the media scrum outside, all those journalists who are desperate to get hold of me – 'The Bunker Woman'. The name the media have given me really sends shivers down my spine.

The first day of the trial is given over to the presentation of the case. The large courtroom is packed with people: judges, jurors, lawyers and prosecutors. I take a deep breath and make my way to my assigned seat. I glance towards the gallery as I hear the murmurs coming from behind. I spot journalists and several media personalities and I don't know how to deal with it all. My knees tremble as I lower myself onto the bench.

Then the doors swing open and I see *him* for the first time since I fled into the interview room at Kungsholmen Police Station. Martin Trenneborg is led in by his lawyer and a few guards. His hands are cuffed in front of him, just as he once restrained me. I cannot control my reaction and I simply break down, crying uncontrollably and shaking wildly. The scarf I am wearing to deflect nosy stares is soon dripping wet. It all comes flooding back as soon as I see him, right there in front of me. My lawyer passes me tissue after tissue but it's a losing battle.

Martin doesn't give anything away when he looks at me, which makes me hate him even more. I keep crying for so long that I find myself with a banging headache. My lawyer hands me a painkiller and to my great relief it is decided that the trial is to be held behind closed doors, so the media are ushered out. My 'breaking down' is still widely reported though.

My eyes are almost swollen shut and that's a sensation I will get used to over the seven long days of the trial. It's an incredibly trying experience. Once the case has been presented and the first day's proceedings are over, I feel exhausted, but above all, I'm grateful that it is out of the way.

*

On day two, the key figures in the trial visit the bunker to get an idea of the scale of the thing and to see exactly what the place where I was held captive looks like. While I feel great relief that I don't have to travel there myself, it does feel as though their seeing it with their own eyes will be for the best. Martin's lawyer is arguing that the trip is unnecessary and I don't blame her: everyone seeing the place with their own eyes will do her client no favours. Anyone with a beating heart inside his chest must surely feel revulsion when confronted with the awful place where he kept me locked up.

By the third day, the day of my testimony, I feel completely exhausted and barely able to think, although I'm as nervous as ever. They lead Martin away when the time comes for me to take the stand and that's a huge relief. I am desperate not to do, or say, anything wrong. Already it feels like lots of people think that I am at least partly to blame for all this because of the work I was doing and I don't want to give the wrong impression. I want them to see and to hear Isabel Eriksson's testimony, straight from the heart, for them not just to be looking at, listening to 'the escort' throughout the proceedings. That's especially true when it comes to the rape. I have to reveal everything – from telling them about my childhood to what it was like working as an escort to how Martin and I met that fateful day. My lawyer has warned me that Martin's defence will come out all guns blazing and I have done my best to steel myself. Despite my best efforts, I can't keep a lid on all those emotions. As soon as I start recounting the detail of how he drugged me, I break down again. In fact, they even call a short break to give me a chance to compose myself before we carry on.

Afterwards, I saw people online mocking me, some of them saying it's impossible to rape someone who works as an escort. That's ridiculous of course, and it made me furious, as well as very sad. I just want everyone who sees and listens to the trial or follows the story to realise that it wasn't 'an escort' who was abducted – it was me, a woman with dreams of my own, with friends, family, plans for the future, with fears and emotions like everyone else. Martin Trenneborg might just as easily have found me on a dating site and drugged me on a perfectly normal date.

This constant pressure to defend myself in front of everyone makes everything much more difficult. Sometimes it feels like there isn't a victim and a perpetrator in this case, but two perpetrators – judging by some of the comments and articles I read online. Martin, on the other hand, is treated much more kindly in the Swedish press than by foreign outlets. In several television programmes he is portrayed as a gentle, confused soul who simply wants to be loved. That really does not reflect the truth of what he subjected me to, for six whole days, days where I didn't know whether I was going to live or die. And this talk about just wanting someone to settle down with really doesn't match the reality – especially since he admitted that he was planning to take more than one woman hostage. I really believe that he gets a kick out of wielding power. That he, for once, is in the driving seat – not like all his previous encounters which have ended with the women leaving him. He wanted to make sure that no one could leave him this time.

My testimony continues after lunch, by which point I'm so worn out that I struggle to go on. My head is still throbbing after all the crying. I feel completely empty; I just want all this to be over. So when the second prosecutor starts asking me questions I can barely summon the energy to respond, I tell them I can't remember. I notice my lawyer getting a bit frustrated, but I really don't have any reserves left to draw on. *This is not good – really not good.* Soon it will be Martin's lawyer's turn to cross-examine me and in this state she's going to steamroller me. So when my lawyer requests another break, the judge's reply is like a gift from above.

'I think we can call it a day there. It has been a difficult and intense experience for all concerned.'

*

The trial reconvenes after the weekend. I've spent it at home, getting some rest for a couple of days, and Mum has come with me to Stockholm on this Monday, the fourth day of the trial. I feel stronger than before, even if Martin's presence in the courtroom does provoke strong reactions at times. I feel better prepared to fight for my right to be heard, to tell the world what an awful thing he did to me. The testimony is a success, at least according to my lawyer, who tells me I've done really well – that I managed to give relevant, concise answers to all the questions asked of me by Trenneborg's lawyer.

After my testimony, the next witness is a doctor called by the defence, who is to explain more about the drugs I was given. I think his lawyer expects the doctor's contribution to benefit Martin's cause, or else she wouldn't have called him as a witness. But it backfires. Not only was I given a potentially lethal dose, far beyond the recommended limit – Martin didn't actually have any of the equipment he would have needed to save me had things gone wrong. I could have died, said the doctor. The risk was quite significant.

My emotions are all over the place as I sit there in the courtroom. On the one hand, it's absurd, sitting there, listening to all these things being said about me; it makes me feel upset and angry. On the other hand, I do feel much calmer knowing that the worst of it – my own testimony – is over, and I can finally begin to relax. I can focus more on what is actually being said.

Later in the trial, when Martin takes the stand, there is no sign of any remorse, not a flicker of empathy for me. He simply recounts – calmly, perfectly composed, detached almost – everything he did to me, then gives some evasive answers about the rape on Saturday and about what things were like for me inside the bunker. It's plain to see that he's doing his best to play down my suffering yet when he's asked about details, about the bunker and its construction, his enthusiasm gets the better of him. On several occasions, the judge asks him to hurry up, that we don't need to hear the minor details, that what he's telling us is simply a waste of time. Martin, though, just looks as calm and unmoved as ever. I try to avoid looking at him as much as possible, but I do happen to make eye contact a few times. He stares straight at me. At one point he sneers over at me, mocking me from his seat.

During the police investigation and the trial itself, a number of terrible things of which I had no idea emerge. A 'sex contract' was found on Martin's computer, detailing his plans to hold several women captive at once, that the standard term of imprisonment will be ten years. If the woman does not agree to, for example, anal sex, another year is to be added to the 'sentence'. Refusing sex in general is to be punished by a hundred-day extension. Any attempt to escape adds five years. He had sketches that proved he planned to keep several people prisoner at once and that he planned to use collective punishment. Those held were to write letters to loved ones, which would then be posted from places all around the world. Despite all of this, his lawyer is still trying to emphasise what a well-liked physician he is, that he studied at a top medical school, how popular he is with both his patients and his colleagues. How he has never been the subject of a formal complaint.

I can see the judge and the jurors' reactions to some of Martin's oddest statements and I can tell that they sympathise with me. They realise what a hellish time I've been through and what a dangerous man Martin Trenneborg really is.

*

On 23 February 2016, five months after I escaped, the verdict arrives. I've spent the past few months just wandering around Uddevalla, waiting. My life has been put on pause and, needless to say, I've stopped working as an escort. There are live broadcasts from the courthouse and all the major papers are covering the story. I, meanwhile, am watching from the sofa, Nellie sitting in my lap as I count down the last minutes. Finally, eleven o'clock arrives. I hold my breath as the reporter states that Martin Trenneborg, known to many as 'The Bunker Doctor', has been sentenced to ten years' imprisonment for abduction, but has been acquitted of rape. I am torn. Ten years is a long time to spend in prison, yet it still troubles me that he wasn't convicted of the rape.

It's only a matter of minutes before the news is all over the internet. There's interest from around the world and of course all Swedish media is giving it coverage. My lawyer calls and warns me to expect Trenneborg's lawyer to lodge an appeal, explains that these high-profile verdicts are nearly always appealed. He says that we might want to consider appealing ourselves. Instinctively I just want to say no. I want to put all this behind me, try to get on with my life. Then, when my lawyer informs me that I wouldn't need to attend court, that I can give him power of attorney, I agree to it: I don't want to let the rape go. Martin Trenneborg told me many times that he had had sex with me while I was drugged unconscious. That he took the condom with him. In the notes I've seen, it says police found a used condom at his place, along with bloody bandages, needles and other things that he used to drug me, yet he still denies it ever happened. I want justice. So I say yes. We appeal.

*

The Court of Appeal agrees with the assessment and deliberations of the District Court, and has no other verdict than that handed down by said court.

I read and re-read the Appeal Court verdict over and over again. The passage is about the rape. The Appeal Court deems, just as the District Court had, that there was insufficient evidence to prove that Martin Trenneborg had sex with me on that Saturday. I am described as credible, that I have given a detailed and consistent account of what happened, while Martin has changed his tune a few times, yet now, when it comes down to my word against his, they come down on his side. They take into account his good behaviour – the fact that he has cooperated fully and described the bunker in detail, despite his basically refusing to talk about his own mental health. He has always tried to play down my suffering and tried to use all sorts of distractions and versions of events that were obviously concocted in hindsight.

The court also finds that abduction normally carries a sentence of ten years' imprisonment, but that Martin was suffering from a psychiatric condition that affected his behaviour. They also state that he is likely to be struck off, that he will not be allowed to work as a doctor, and rule that this should also be 'taken into account when considering his punishment'.

The prosecutor had argued for fifteen or sixteen years' imprisonment, while Martin's lawyer tried to get the District Court's sentence reduced. To my dismay, the Appeal Court agrees – eight years instead of ten. I just can't believe it. My insides are in turmoil and the tears flow freely as I read their decision. Of course it's obvious to anyone that Martin Trenneborg has some kind of psychiatric illness. How else could anyone drug and abduct somebody, and plan to keep them in a bunker which they'd spent five years constructing? The question is whether he is so disturbed that he doesn't know right from wrong. I don't think so, and neither does the court, because otherwise they would have had to sentence him to a secure hospital and attached special conditions to determine whether he could be released. He was sent to an ordinary prison.

Martin Trenneborg is a psychopath, in my view: a very intelligent psychopath. I subsequently found out that he had been a member of Mensa. How the psychiatric condition to which the Appeal Court referred – suicidal thoughts and depression – can cut two years off his sentence is beyond me. Lots of people battle with depression, but they don't go round drugging and kidnapping people, or take them to purpose-built bunkers. I believe his being struck off was what was really on the Appeal Court's mind, and that angers me greatly. What has that got to do with the crime? Are they saying that it's another punishment, above and beyond the jail time? Why not go a bit further and lop off another few years? After all, chances are he's going to be associated with this for the rest of his life. Whose fault is it that Martin Trenneborg is going to have his licence to practise medicine revoked? That's right – his own. The moment he made up his mind to commit this terrible crime he also gave up the right to the trust that we as a society give to our doctors. I doubt the sentence would have been cut had it been a bus driver who had kidnapped me. No one explaining that 'he probably won't be allowed to drive a bus when he gets out'. Is his sentencing down to his respected title? Not only is it wrong, it's pure speculation. He will 'probably' be stripped of his licence. If that turns out to be wrong, will they then lock him up again for another couple of years?

The judgment goes on to explain that the sentence was reduced because he decided to stop of his own accord. I really cannot see it that way. If the keys to my flat had worked, if there hadn't been a note from the police on my door, then maybe I would still be sitting in there. To quote CNN, 'She only escaped through a series of unlikely events.' The Appeal Court also rules that the crime ended when I left the bunker. That's not my view at all. It wasn't until I stepped into that interview room, with a policeman at my side, that I felt anything like free. I think it's fair to say that in many ways I may never feel free again.

I sit on the sofa feeling extremely restless and not knowing what to do with myself. Then, surfing through online coverage of the case, I come across this:

> *The prosecutor's demand for the demolition of the structure in which the woman was held, a bunker-like utility building, was rejected by the court.*

My head is spinning. He's been given eight years inside. In 2021, Martin Trenneborg can roam the streets of Sweden as a free man. He can return to his farmhouse in Skåne to think about what he might fill his life with, since he can no longer work as a doctor.

And he won't even have to destroy his bunker.

*

During the trial, and since, Nellie and I have had to learn to live with what we experienced. I have noticed that I find it most difficult if things are too quiet. If it's too dark, I feel the same way. When I'm trying to get to sleep, I tend to put the telly or the radio on in another room and I always have a light on somewhere. At first I was waking up several times a night, soaked in sweat and gasping as the anxiety laid itself over my chest like a lead weight. I didn't know where I was. For long periods, I've been given sleeping pills to help me settle at night and I have been treated for post-traumatic stress disorder (PTSD). I have been struck by panic attacks when my fridge has unexpectedly clicked into life, just as the one in the bunker did that time, when I got my hopes up that there might be people outside. *That sound.* The compressor kicking in ... It's so weird, the sort of things that can set you off. To begin with, I was struck by a terrible panic and both my thoughts and my emotions were right back in the darkness and the dust of the bunker. Now that a little time has passed, things are getting better, but that sound still makes me very uneasy if I happen to hear it. The same thing happens with heavy doors opening and closing. It takes me back: sitting there, listening out for the doors, the terror I felt every time I heard his footsteps approaching. I still have nightmares, and the great outdoors – something I've loved as long as I can remember – now feels scary and unfamiliar because I'm reminded of the woods around the bunker. Every time I see a house or an outhouse that looks like Martin's, my stomach ties itself in knots and I have become so claustrophobic that I can't even sleep with the door closed anymore. Seeing a doctor is even worse. I know how irrational it is, but every time I have an appointment, particularly if the doctor is male, I am wracked with anxiety. If a man reminds my of Martin Trenneborg – appearance, build, mannerisms or voice – complete panic overwhelms me. This despite my knowing that he's in prison now. I don't even want to think about what it will be like when he gets out.

I am in therapy, and I hope one day that the plucky, fearless Isabel will be back. I really hope she's in here somewhere. I really like her. Maybe this book is a step along the way.

And Nellie, my beautiful, darling Nellie … She was never the same again. After her experiences in the bunker she became aggressive, especially if I was lying in bed or on the sofa and someone came into the room. She would bark wildly and try to bite and then growl like she was possessed. She would get in the same state if she heard noises at night. I spoke to an expert on dog behaviour, who told me that she was probably trying to protect me after having seen me being treated badly and after detecting my intense fear. The thought of her having to live the rest of her life like that was heartbreaking. She is no longer with us. Because of the behaviours she developed after our time in the bunker, she was involved in an accident and died. Thinking about her tears me apart and I miss her every day.

'Did you ever think about taking your own life?'

I have been asked that many times. The answer though is that no, I never did. It never even occurred to me. I wasn't ever going to give up: I was going to get Nellie and I out of there.

EPILOGUE

There are three reasons for this book's existence.

First of all, I wanted the chance to tell the world, in my own words and without the media's twisting of the facts, what actually happened. The abduction. The time inside the bunker. What it was like to sit there, not knowing where I was, whether I was going to survive the day, or even who it was that had abducted me. I want to tell people what a living hell that was. Not least because so many people express opinions about how it 'wasn't that bad'. Martin Trenneborg's lawyer submitted an application for a new trial to the Supreme Court. It is a prime example of what I am talking about. This is the bulletin from a leading Swedish press agency:

> *Bunker Doctor appeals to Supreme Court*
> *   The doctor convicted of drugging, abducting and then imprisoning a young woman in a bunker has appealed to the Supreme Court to have the verdict overturned. The*

appeal explains that he aims to 'significantly reduce' the length of his sentence.

In September last year, the thirty-eight-year-old met a woman and decided that he would lock her up and keep her as his 'girlfriend'. He drugged the woman before driving her from Stockholm to his farmhouse in Skåne, where he kept her locked up for six days.

The District Court sentenced the doctor to ten years' imprisonment for abduction. The Appeal Court then reduced the sentence on the grounds of diminished responsibility — the man has a psychiatric disorder, which contributed to his behaviour. The thirty-eight-year-old's lawyer, Mari Schaub, maintains that this was still too harsh and will now appeal the verdict.

Schaub hopes the Supreme Court will revisit both the sentence itself — ten years — and how parole will be calculated. The doctor voluntarily released his captive after six days, and has subsequently been struck off — he will no longer be allowed to work as a doctor.

The other element Schaub hopes will be re-examined is the charge itself — abduction — a crime which the Crown Court deemed to have been committed when the doctor abducted the woman with the intent to cause her injury as the legal papers put it.

Were my client's plans for what he wanted to do with the victim really going to cause her injury, as the law states? He has explained that he hoped to have sexual intercourse with her, but only if she wanted to, according to Schaub.

EPILOGUE

In the appeal document, Schaub also describes how the doctor had 'taken several measures to improve the victim's conditions' in what he himself has referred to as a bunker – originally intended as an air-raid shelter. The woman was allowed her dog for company, for example.

He even took the dog for walks, Schaub commented.

In other words: Martin Trenneborg didn't hurt me badly enough even to warrant the punishment handed down by the Crown Court. And besides, he walked my dog.

I am lost for words. Genuinely, completely, lost for words. Only someone completely lacking in empathy could say that he didn't hurt me 'enough' or that what happened to me 'wasn't that bad'. Or perhaps someone who hasn't been given a clear, accurate account of what went on, what it was actually like. That is what I wanted this book to be.

Finally the verdict was delivered – the Supreme Court dismissed the appeal, which means that at least the legal part of this nightmare is finally over for good. It also emerged later on that the reason the bunker wasn't demolished – and, in fact, why it's still cordoned off – is because police are investigating possible earlier crimes. So far, though, the prosecutor is not giving anything away.

Writing this book has also been a form of therapy for me, a way of working through it all. Thinking about what happened and getting it down on the page: what it was like, how I felt, what I think about it now. Perhaps this book will make it a bit easier to put it behind me, now that I feel I've really had my say, and my story is out there in black and white.

I also wanted to talk about my former career and to be open about it. Get rid of some of the prejudices I know exist – ones I used to have myself. I know that many people immediately assume that I must have come from a broken home; that I must have been abused, neglected or assaulted, but that is simply not the case. My childhood was perfectly normal, boringly average.

What I hope to get across to people is what I have learned over the years: that the variety of people working as strippers or escorts is as wide as in any other line of work – we're all different.

At this point there is one thing I do need to make clear, though: I'm talking about people who have chosen that line of work of their own free will. I am well aware that there are many hidden, dark and horrific elements to the industry. There are people who are forced into it. Or perhaps feel that they don't have a choice. People feeding their addictions or punishing themselves. People smuggling. Child prostitution. Pimps selling bodies as if they were possessions, not living human beings. All of that is already out there. It's all already illegal, and I believe that's the way things should stay.

I did choose my own path, and I really did enjoy it. I was able to choose *when* I was going to work, *how much* I worked and – perhaps most importantly – I could choose exactly which clients I wanted to meet and which I did not.

I got that right every time – except once.

EPILOGUE

*

I'm on the road to recovery. I'm still alive. I have a future and a supportive family. I never broke down completely. That psychopath is not going to have the last word when it comes to my health or my life. No way!

I look at the world around me and I'm so grateful to be alive. I positively enjoy all those things that I used to take for granted – feeling fresh air fill my lungs, or the wind and the sun's rays on my face. Birdsong on a summer's day. Being able to go wherever I want, whenever it takes my fancy; to meet whomever I feel like meeting. Not being at the mercy of someone else.

I will stand tall again.

THANK YOU

The journey from a story to a book involves many, many people, especially when the story is as heavy as mine has been.

I want to thank my mum and my sister for their constant warmth and support; my friend Nathalie, who wouldn't give up and made sure that the police kept up their efforts to find out what had happened to me.

My darling Nellie, so sorely missed – thank you for those days and nights of silent comfort when you were at my side. We'll meet again, I'm sure of that.

Thanks also to Father Martin, for all your precious support.

I want to express my gratitude to my Swedish publisher, Lind & Co, and my agents, Nordin Agency, for believing in the book from the start and for treating me so well along the way.

I am so grateful for this second chance at life, each and every day. And this time round, I am not going to blow it.